BLACK ROBE

THE KEMPO/KAJUKENBO CONNECTION

BY
DAVID TAVARES

COPYRIGHT INFORMATION

BLACK ROBE: THE KEMPO/KAJUKENBO CONNECTION
by David Tavares.
Editing and preparation for publication by Zach Royer.

© 2017 All rights reserved.

www.StoneCompassPress.com/titles
www.Black-Robe.net

ISBN: 979-8985929331

First Edition. Revised September 2022.
Written in Oahu, Hawai'i, and printed in the United States of America.

Back Cover Translation: *"The way of the fist - strength from within."*

Published by Stone Compass Press. Our books may be purchased in bulk for promotional, educational, or business use. No portion of this book may be reproduced in any form without permission from the publisher, except as permitted by U.S. copyright law. For permissions contact: www.stonecompasspress.com.

Please note that the author and publisher of this book are NOT RESPONSIBLE in any manner whatsoever for any injury that may result from practicing the techniques and/or following the instructions given within. Since the physical activities described herein may be too strenuous for some readers to engage in safely, a physician must be consulted before training.

STONE COMPASS PRESS

10 9 8 7 6 5 4 3 2 1

TABLE OF CONTENTS

Tribute to Sijo Emperado
Kajukenbo Prayer
Dedication
Acknowledgments
Foreword
Author's Note

1	Introduction…………………………………..	1
2	Godin's Kula Ona Kupale……………….....	7
3	The Hammer and the Anvil………………...	13
4	Young Joe the Forgotten Emperado………..	21
5	Four in the Shadows…………………….....	51
6	The Rising Sun……………………………..	71
7	Total Recall………………………………..	81
8	Effective Kempo/Kajukenbo Street Defense..	87
9	Final Thoughts……………………………..	117
	About the Author…………………………..	124

TRIBUTE TO SIJO EMPERADO

For your paramount contribution to the art of Kajukenbo. The disciples of Kempo and Kajukenbo the world over salute the Kempo/Kajukenbo bow to you Sijo. *Aloha Ke Akua.*

KAJUKENBO
Self-Defense Institute

"THE KAJUKENBO KID"

What's that you say, Mac?
What's wrong with my back?
Well, gather close, buddy, and I'll tell you,
a story of Kajukenbo students and what we go through.

We meet every Tuesday, Wednesday and Thursday night,
to study Kenpo, for use in a fight.
What did you say? What's the use?
Brother, ever see a real Kenpo man on the loose?

First we bow and cleanse our minds,
then get ready for the knocks and grinds,
A smack! A Yell! the class has begun,
the Kenpo squat, and Buster, it's no fun.

We squat and squat all aching with pain,
the muscles and tendons shaking with strain,
and just when we think it's time for a blower,
the instructor says calmly, c'mon "Squat lower."

The minutes tick on and nothing is said,
but each man thinks, "I wish I was dead."
Just to squat, you say, is of nothing to tell,
you're wrong, a ten minute squat is an eternity in hell.
The exercises then start, one by one,
"Come on, make noise, you son of a gun",
We Ha! and Sa! and Hi! and Kiai!
The sweat just pouring, while our fists fly.

The arms are like lead, the legs like jelly,
but still we plug on, got to take off that belly,
then pushups, and situps, neck raises galore,
the leg raises and medicine ball to finish the chore.

Then comes rolls and tumbles the rest of the night,
got to practice hard, got to get it right,
the falls and the counters we've got to learn,
that Black Belt takes years that had to be earned.

So, you ask what's wrong with my back,
and why don't I spend the night in my sack?
Why, there's nothing wrong, I'm all right,
no sack for me, Kenpo class tonight!

Mel Young Ordonez
Age 10

KAJUKENBO PRAYER

Almighty and eternal God. Protector of all who put their trust in thee. Accept the humble homage of our faith and love to thee the one true God. Bless our efforts to preserve the integrity of our United States, a nation founded on Christian principles. Enlighten our rules, guide our law makers. And protect the sanctity of our homes. And bless our efforts in these exercises. Whose sole purpose is developing our bodies. To keep others mindful of thy commandments. Give us perseverance in our actions. That we may use this as the means to be closer to you, the one true God. In the name of thy beloved son, Jesus Christ, our lord. Amen.

-Grandmaster Frank Ordonez
10th-degree Co-founder Kajukenbo, Wake Island 1958

DEDICATION

For my daughter *Toni-Marie,*
and my grand children *Cheylene-Faith*, *Xavier,* and *Kainoa.*
Without all of you, I would be empty.

Two great martial arts legends. The great Mas Oyama, founder of Kyokushin Karate and the great Frank Ordonez, Co-Founder of Kajukenbo at the Honolulu International Airport, 1960

ACKNOWLEDGMENTS

Since the birth of martial arts, countries, and cultures from all over the planet created their distinct style in the art of combat. From the Temples of Shaolin to the dojos in Japan. Each combatant was dedicated and loyal to the particular style and philosophy of their art. Each fighter believed their one-dimensional style was superior to their opponent. It would take thousands of years for one man to believe differently and forever break down the barrier of the martial arts wall. He would recruit five men who shared the same philosophy as he did. Four were able to journey with him on this long and narrow disciplined road.

To Uncle Frank Ordonez. Without your vision, there would be no Kajukenbo.

FOREWORD

I still remember the night my mother had to come in and watch an entire two-hour martial arts class before the owner of the school would let me join. The school was located on Kaimuki Avenue. It was upstairs of a dry cleaners store and a bakery. It was 1962 and I was almost eleven years old. That was the beginning of my life long relationship with Professor Walter L.N. Godin.

Professor Godin was a real enigma. I remember him being very proud of the fact that he got his students to pray at least twice a day when they came to class. We would say the Kajukenbo school prayer at both the beginning and the end of every class. Yet our classes were brutal and challenging both physically and mentally. We were exhausted, bruised, bloodied messes, usually standing in horse stances over puddles of our sweat.

He taught me about being humble.

I once asked him as a young boy, "*When can I go for my purple belt test?*" He replied, "*Tiger* (he called me Tiger all the time), *you just earned the right to call yourself a white belt in Kajukenbo and not have that be a piece of string to hold your gi closed.*"

From that moment on I learned NEVER to ask for a belt test or a promotion.

Godin once told me that he did everything to the excessive, whether it was martial arts or anything else. He lived by that rule for good or bad, that was the man he was. I miss him.

I am honored to be a part of this book about my Kajukenbo teacher. He is one of the most famous or infamous black belts in the Kajukenbo system. This book covers the beginning of Professor Godin's training in the Palama Settlement, his training with Joe Emperado, and most importantly, what happened on that fateful night at The Pink Elephant Bar on that Memorial Day weekend in 1958.

A warrior in his right, the author David Tavares has spent untold hours researching documents, interviewing honorable martial artists, and using Professor Godin's own words to compile this informative, yet potentially controversial book.

A must-read for the serious martial artist who wants to be educated in Kempo/Kajukenbo history.

-Eugene R. Sedeno
Senior Grandmaster, Kajukenbo

AUTHOR'S NOTE

"Outcasts learn to thrive on being hated."
-Mike Norton, <u>Fighting for Redemption</u>

Why the title <u>Black Robe</u>? I once asked Professor Godin the question of why we wear black gis as opposed to white. He told me Professor Mitose wore a black gi and Professor Chow later when he went on wore black. He thinks Chow wore black because of the Chinese influence in Kempo. Gung Fu stylists mostly wore black in their training. Chow had some Gung Fu background and was proud of his Chinese heritage. He believed it was to set us apart from the traditional Japanese white Karate gi. Some Kempo schools still use the white gi. Professor Marino Tiwanak's CHA three Kempo color belts wear white gis until they reach the black belt level. The instructors

Author in his black robe, 1972

wear black as they did in the early Kajukenbo days. Godin said there is no concrete proof of any single or rational reason for the black gi, at least that he knows of. Many people may have their reasons or speculations, but he wasn't sure. He did say though that the black gi did fit the reputation of the Kempo and Kajukenbo fighters. Back in the late 50s and 60s, the Hawaii Karate Congress was the major organization for bringing martial arts schools in Hawaii together for tournament competition. The congress and the tournament competitors were dominated largely by the Japanese Karate style. The Kempo and Kajukenbo style was looked upon as black sheep or rebels of the martial arts because of the mixed styles involved that were mostly suited for the streets, and not tournament point fighting competition. While traditional Karate on the other hand, in its pure form, focuses more on the beauty and the form of its movements in the art. Their tournament strategy was more focused on countering the opponent waiting for him to attack, then countering with one clean shot for a point.

The Kempo and Kajukenbo fighter has a more aggressive style of a continuous two-fisted attack followed up with kicks (sometimes elbows) even after a point was scored, at many times rushing the Karate stylist out of the ring. For this reason, most were disqualified for excessive contact or unsportsmanlike conduct, and thereby they were looked upon as aggressive, undisciplined outcasts in the Hawaii tournament circuit as well as the Hawaii martial arts community. But THE ONE theory Professor Godin liked the best and told me with a sly smile, was a phrase one of his friends who was a black belt in Shotokan once told him.

"You Kempo guys show up to the tournaments wearing black gis like you going to a funeral..." Godin added, *"white gis funeral! "*

-David Tavares, Black Robe

http://www.Black-Robe.net

INTRODUCTION

"The less a man knows, the easier it is to convince him he knows everything."
-Anonymous

If you bought this book or even piqued your interest to open it and read it, then you and I have a martial arts connection in the Kempo or Kajukenbo lineage. Our style evolved (Kempo) and was born (Kajukenbo) in the Hawaiian Islands. This means with your Kempo or Kajukenbo training you have a direct connection to me and the Hawaiian Islands.

Hawaii has played a major role in introducing our art the world over. With men like Ed Parker, Tony Ramos, Aleju Reyes, and many more it would be impossible to acknowledge them all. Mitose and Chow are credited for putting Kempo on the Hawaii martial arts map. Mitose taught his family's style Kosho-Ryu Kenpo. Chow incorporated Gung-Fu into his blend of Kara-Ho Kempo. Adriano Emperado is the most celebrated icon in the Kajukenbo system, if you mention the art of Kajukenbo the first name that comes to mind IS Adriano Emperado. All three men have volumes of printed publications and articles written about them many times over. I want to write a little about the unsung heroes who stood in the shadows but played a very influential part in the Kempo and Kajukenbo world. Peter Choo, Joe Holk, George Chang, and the man who spearheaded the incorporation of these men's styles to make it one, Frank Ordonez, and also young Joe Emperado and his student and friend, Walter

Godin.

What happened that fateful Memorial Day weekend in the early morning hours at The Pink Elephant bar back in 1958?

Professor Godin granted me his only interview through Fighting Arts Hawaii magazine back in 2001, as told by the people directly involved that night through the original police transcripts that Professor Godin let me read during the interview. Throughout history, Kempo/Kajukenbo stylists were conditioned to believe that Godin was a coward and ran away leaving Joe to die. Some say to get help, others say to save his skin. When you read what one of the attackers said about his running away, you will find that history sometimes is what those of influence want it to be.

Tommy Lam working Muay Thai drills with former UFC welterweight contender Jason "Mayhem" Miller.

Most of the book will be about Kempo and Kajukenbo stylists and their particular mixed or traditional style of effective self-defense, and a bit of my 46-year experience in training and learning effective martial arts with the martial artist that I have trained with, spoken to, or interviewed. I consider myself a student of martial arts. Kempo is my foundation. Kajukenbo is my roots. I learned from most of my Kajukenbo brothers that without Kempo you would cut the head off the Kajukenbo system. Kempo is the primary style in Kajukenbo.

To all who have taught me effective martial arts, I thank you.

Professor Godin, I credit my Kempo skills to you.

He had the balls to change his method from traditional style to his blend of Kempo and added the full contact fighting style to it in the early 70s during the pioneering full contact fighting days.

My older brothers Donald Dennison and Gilbert Tavares, both boxers, taught me western boxing which helped me with the full-contact style transition.

The late Tony Rodriguez, who was my boxing trainer at Kalakaua gym, took me to win the 1983 USA/ABF state flyweight title.

Tommy Lam, whom I am indebted to in martial arts and life. Before my martial arts school failed, Tommy always opened his doors to my students and me and taught us Brazilian Ju-Jitsu, and when my school closed for good he welcomed me to keep training at his school. Without him and the Kempo Unlimited organization, I would have had no one to train with.

Danny Lam, who drilled me with focus mitt training that I never saw before. My former boxing trainer Tony Rodriguez trained boxers at the highest level and worked the focus mitts with me as well as former WBC Jr. Lightweight Champion, Rolondo Naverette. Danny humbled me making me realize that my mind was not full when it came to my stand-up fighting skills.

Professor James Jowers, went out of his way to contact me when I started school and invited my students and me to come and work out with him and Tommy at Kempo Unlimited. His single unselfish act would change my martial arts life forever.

To the self-defense practitioners who helped me to illustrate your method of effective self-defense - big MAHALOS.

To Andrew Evans, who used his librarian skills to help articulate my expressions on paper, much aloha, and Eugene Sedeno, who wrote the foreword, you just elevated the book ten-fold.

To my former students who continued to train with me when I left another Kempo school that I taught at Ernie Wakugawa, Kimo Sanders, Nohea Sanders, and Tracy Woita. Much mahalo.

To my families, both Tavares and Dennison, who encouraged my martial arts training, and especially to my Mom who enrolled me in Godin's Kula Ona Kupale Pacific Palisades branch in June of 1971 when it all started. I love you, Mom.

And to you for reading this book, thank you.

The way is in training...keep training.

Chief Instructor Godin and student Martin Buell, Head Instructor of the Palisades branch, 1972

GODIN'S KULA ONA KUPALE 1971

"The journey is the reward."

-Lao Tzu

Saturday morning cartoons were always the best way to start the weekend. I always sat in front of the TV in our family room eating cereal and watching everything from the *Jetsons* to *Fearless Fly*.

Now it's different.

My recently divorced mom signed me up for Kempo. Saturday morning training started at 9:00 am. It was 8:30, and I needed to walk to the Palisades Rec. Center, where a guy named Godin had Chinese Kempo classes. I didn't want to go, I didn't know anyone and I was new to the neighborhood.

Before class, the head instructor of the branch, Martin Buell, informed us that Chief Instructor Godin will be there later on. *"So train hard and look sharp,"* he says. *Godin? The guy on the patch?* I asked myself. The club patch had a black hooded Dharuma sitting in a Buddha position. I wondered if that was who he was referring to.

After we did the club prayer and the warm-ups, the head instructor had us do basics from the squatting position. I'm in the back row. White belts and shitty students always get put in the back. I'm near the entrance where I can hear taps from shoes.

The training area and entrance at the recreation center are separated by tall bushes so I can't see who is entering, but as I looked down behind me, I saw shiny high-heeled boots through the bottom stems of the bush and heard taps with each step. I saw another person following him, wearing lady-dress shoes. I turned and looked up over my left shoulder and saw him entering. He's standing near me, while I'm in a half-squatting stance. I slowly looked up and saw the glass-shined black boots, black flared double knit pants, and a black and white checked gi top, one that resembled Joe Lewis' gi top from his point fighting days. He wore a plain black belt with no Chinese characters printed on it. He wore a gold wedding band on his ring finger and a gold jade ring on his pinky. The pinky finger caught my eye. It was long and filed to a sharp point. I would later learn he used it for gouging and raking eyes during his debt-collecting days. He had fairly long black hair with Elvis-style sideburns.

I was underdeveloped as a kid and was very short for my age.

Godin, when I looked up to see his face, looked eight feet tall. He had thick black eyebrows and dark eyes that stared right through you. He didn't seem to realize me looking at him. When he stood at the entrance the head instructor stopped the class and had us all face Godin and introduced him as the Chief Instructor and gave him our respect with the Kempo bow.

Usually, when our class would end I would go down to the rec. center playground and mess around on the playground equipment that was available, but I overheard a couple of the adults say that Chief Godin was going to teach street defense in their class, so I stayed and waited to watch the adult class. After warm-ups, Godin used one of the higher-ranking students as a partner, Gilbert Ragudo, who was a brown belt at the time. Gilbert incidentally fought the great Howard Jackson to a draw in the 1974 Hawaii vs. Mainland tournament, with a 5-5 even score. Gilbert punched and the rest was a blur. Godin's cat-like reflexes and speed were too quick for anyone, especially a nine-year-old kid. All I saw and heard was Godin's high-pitched scream and a combination of blows and a takedown, followed by repeated hammer blows to the face and groin. Ragudo got back up when it was over. But Godin wanted to show the defense again to the adults, slower but still with power. Before he threw the punch again Gilbert looked like a man about to be executed, walking his last walk. Doing the same technique again without the takedown, dropping him instead with a short blow to the solar plexus. This time Godin did not follow up with the repeated hammer strikes to the face and groin. Instead with a stomp to Gilbert's head just past shy of the side of his temple stomping the floor with his high heel boot. Godin wanted to show the variations of the technique when applying it. After he explained the techniques, he had the rest of the class practice the defense.

After witnessing Chief Godin in action I walked home thinking, "*Godin...that's a bad Mutha fa!*"

Me in the second row far right next to Martin Buell. Kneeling are
Bill Takeuchi (left) and Gilbert Ragudo (right). Chief Godin is standing far left.

1973 class photo. I'm in front second from left.
Godin far right is now a Professor and sports a red gi top.

Advance youth class with instructors. Me front row second from left again.

Professor Godin at a Lima Lama tournament, 1975

THE HAMMER AND THE ANVIL

"My best description of the Kajukenbo style, I see Kempo as the anvil of the Kajukenbo system...and Godin is the hammer."
-10th Degree Professor Kimo Ferriea of the Kempo Jutsu Kai Schools

"Before Godin-No Godin-After Godin-No Godin"
-David Tavares

In 1952 a young Walter Godin walked into the Palama settlement Kajukenbo training area, a place unparalleled in developing the fiercest street fighters in the Hawaiian Islands territory. At just 15 years of age, he would learn the world's first mixed martial arts style, the art of Kajukenbo.

He would befriend a young man who was not only his instructor but a man whom he looked up to and loved as an older brother and who would forever change his fighting skills and his life. The two men's names would also forever be linked and sealed in fate in Kajukenbo history. Young Joe would forever be remembered as a martial arts shooting star, lent to us from God for a moment in time, and Godin as the most controversial figure in the Kajukenbo realm.

Growing up on Richard Lane in Kalihi, Hawaii back in the '40s and '50s meant come hard or don't come. Walter Leo Niakala Godin had to live hard his entire adolescent life. With countless street fights and street hustling. He saw the worst Kalihi Valley had to offer and needed street smarts and street fighting skills to survive the hostile aggressive life.

Coming from a pedigree of martial arts, his father of French ancestry taught young Walter his country's kickboxing art of Savate. Walter, who was already using his kicking ability in the streets, thought his father was refining what they called in the Hawaii streets a "shoe job." Kicking the man you were fighting with, when he was down in the streets, was known as a "shoe job." And Godin was now able to shoe job anyone, anywhere on the human anatomy with finesse, while they were standing or down.

Having a private school education at the Kamehameha schools, Godin was rejected in his neighborhood and became a prime target as prey by the predominant public school kids. Using his father's Savate discipline and Judo from "Rubber man" Migami, he learned at age 12 that having the size, street intellect, and fighting skills gave him a big advantage over his would-be adversaries. Taking on and defeating a would-be mob job at times. A young Godin realized early he liked inflicting damage on others who sought harm toward him.

At age 15, he would watch a martial arts movie with one of his friends at an old movie theater in Chinatown, Honolulu. "Lightning Karate" or something of the sort he recalled. Watching the outnumbered martial artist destroy his attackers immediately caught the attention of the 15-year-old Godin. *"That guy is just like me."* he thought. *"If I could learn to fight like that. I'd be more dangerous and I won't need trash can lids or sticks and rocks to beat these guys."*

On the bus ride home, he kept repeating the fight scenes in his head. Hearing his friend talk, but hardly paid attention. *"I got to find me a Karate school!"* he told himself. After asking and looking around, someone in the neighborhood told him Palama Settlement had a Karate school. It did not take long for the youngster to hop on the bus and head to Palama. Much to his dismay, the sessions were closed door. But that did not deter the young Godin, who would go three times a week to see if he could get a glance at the training but would only be able to see the martial artists exiting the old building where they trained and hung out and talked story with each other, as Walter would hang around to see if anyone would talk to him or ask him what his business there was. All would ignore his presence.

It would one day take Charles Lakalo, one of the black belts who was spotting Joe Emperado as he was lifting weights hours before class started, to recognize the youngster's existence. *"Come here, give me a hand spotting him,"* the elder Lakalo said to the surprised Godin.

Godin jumped and helped with what was needed. *"You need help with anything else?"* he asked when he was through spotting Joe.

"What you doing always hanging around here after we pau class?" Joe asked.

"I wanted to train and learn from you guys if can," replied Godin.

"Bullshit! You gonna get your ass kicked and run home to your mom boy." Joe barked. *"And we no take kids,"* he added.

"I'm not afraid!" Godin was quick to answer.

Joe looked at the teen, gave a slight smile, then laughed and said, *"I'll see what I can do."*

When he returned for Tuesday's training, his heart was pounding, and his spirit was anxious. Joe let him in the training area doors. Walking through the doors, the young Godin had no idea of the sadistic training and life-changing experiences he was in for. In the training area, he saw men in white and black uniforms. Watching them train in a military-like manner, Joe (in black) sounded the commands and the white uniforms followed. You could hear a pin drop at times, then a loud *kiai* from the students in unison that echoed in the building. The group then paired up and did self-defense tricks. Watching each student defend against an attack and beat the shit out of their downed opponent.

The young Godin stood in awe. *"This is what I need. This is what I want to learn!"* he told himself.

As sweat bled through every pore of his body, he tried desperately to keep up and follow along with each exercise. There was no prejudice or favoritism in these men. They hammered him and put him through a repetitious grind like any other adult.

A shaven-headed Godin.

It had been a year into training now. Sixteen-year-old Walter Godin was a more skilled martial artist, disciplined, focused, stronger, tougher and a lot street cockier. He earned his badge and strutted knowing he belonged to a group of elite fighting machines. Being accepted in their realm was an extraordinary occurrence, especially as a youngster. Kajukenbo students, as well as instructors, were notorious for weeding out the soft or weaker students or potential students. With no acceptance from other martial artists from different schools, Godin, still, a white belt, was setting his goal and proving his worth to make it to the purple belt. Kajukenbo at the time had no testing curriculum. When the instructors felt you were ready for the next level, you were promoted.

During one training session, in which one of the occasional times Adriano showed up to the Palama class when class was over, Joe had a ritual where all the students would attack him one after the other. When Godin became a regular he would always be the first. *Getting your ass kicked over with is a lot better than watching others than waiting and anticipating yours. I learned that quickly.*

When Joe was done he had everyone line back up, then he yelled out *"Walter Godin! Front and center!"*

Adriano opened his folder and pulled out a piece of paper that resembled a certificate. Godin's eyes lit up and he fell out of ranks as a soldier would out of formation. He stood front and center at the head of the class facing the other black belts. Joe and Adriano were standing next to each other. With butterflies in his stomach, Godin crossed his forearms together, snapping his gi loudly. He then pumped both fists downward, snapping his gi once again, standing in an informal position, eyes darting, staring straight ahead.

"This is it," Godin told himself. Godin now peered at Joe, whose head was down in a bow-like position, staring at the floor below. *"Walter Godin,"*

Adriano continued, *"for selling the most Portuguese sausages in our fundraiser."*

Godin's eyebrows raised. He looked once again at Joe, who now had his chin buried deep in his chest, shoulders hunched over. Godin could see Joe's shoulders now bouncing up and down, trying desperately to hold back his uncontrollable laugh.

"The Kajukenbo Self-Defense Institute would like to present you with this certificate of appreciation," Adriano concluded.

Godin stood there, staring blankly.

"Fundraiser?" he thought. *"Selling the most sausages? Certificate of appreciation?!"* …Mother fa!!!

Godin going out in style.

One bad bill collector!

Young Joe's grave photo shows the ravages of time since that fateful day 59 years ago.

YOUNG JOE
THE FORGOTTEN EMPERADO

"We are all immortal until our work on earth here is done."
-George Whitefield, 1714-1770

"Nothing is better than listening to a lie...when you already know the truth."
-Portuguese proverb

Our Beloved Joseph Directo Emperado was buried in Honolulu, Hawai'i

To train in Kajukenbo is to know the history of Kajukenbo. A history passed down from generation to generation, from instructor to student, which includes details from books, DVDs, the Internet, and information about the beginnings of the five founders who pioneered the art of Kajukenbo to the progressive present state of the system. However, the most mysterious, complex, and disputable segment of Kajukenbo history is young Professor Joe's demise. Multitudes have been told second-hand stories of Joe Emperado on how his life was cut short from this world, stories that were inconsistent or incomplete, and some even being a taboo subjects to speak of in the presence of Kajukenbo elders. No one but Joe Emperado and Walter Godin and the Godin family knows the facts of that fateful night, facts that have been largely hidden for nearly 60 years.

I have heard people say my instructor Walter Godin ran from the three assailants when one of the attackers, George Shimabuku, pulled the knife that ended the life of Professor Joe. Also, stories that he ran to get help. Others have told stories that hours before the incident Kajukenbo black belts were in the Pink Elephant bar drinking and talking with Joe and Godin, then later leaving to go home, insisting that Joe would still have been alive today had they stayed.

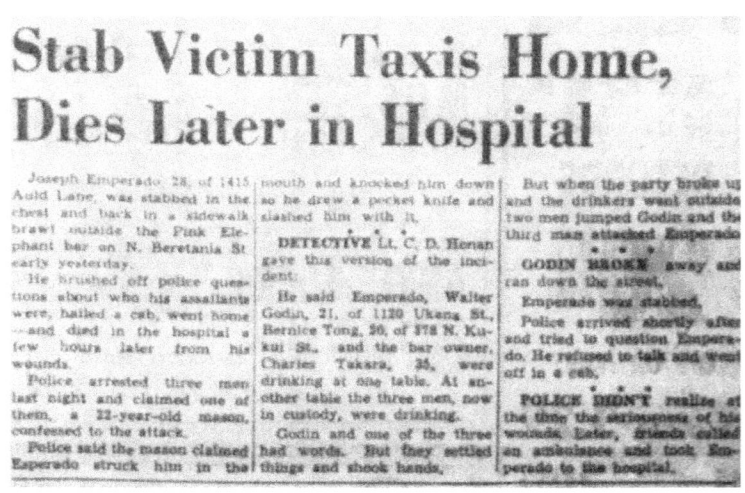

Stories upon stories until Y2K, when Professor Godin granted me an interview on his life in the martial arts, his involvement with organized crime, drugs, and his incarceration. But most important, on a spiritual side how he turned his life around and surrendered his soul to God. But the point of his life I needed to know about and I thought the Kempo and Kajukenbo world needs to know to fill that void are the facts, the truth of what went down that early morning hours on Friday, May 30th, 1958.

The writings that are forthcoming are facts from the original police transcripts that Professor Godin showed to me during the interview. I was also shown pictures of the crime scene, photos of the three assailants, and other photos that I will not discuss.

It will set the record straight of my instructor's reputation to many. But there will be many others who will still hold to their beliefs and what they were taught or told or conditioned to believe. No matter what proof is given to them, they will still interpret the truth in their way.

Professor Godin once told me, *"In the martial arts, when people hear my name, in their mind, they have already made a decision about what they think of me, but I'm not bothered by it."*

As states in the Bible, John 8:32, *"For ye shall know the truth, and the truth will set you free."*

I will also write afterthoughts as to fact vs. fiction at the end of the chapter, and I will include the important facts of the witness' statements. Other details may take up too many pages of this publication, but I will go into more detail about them in a possible upcoming DVD.

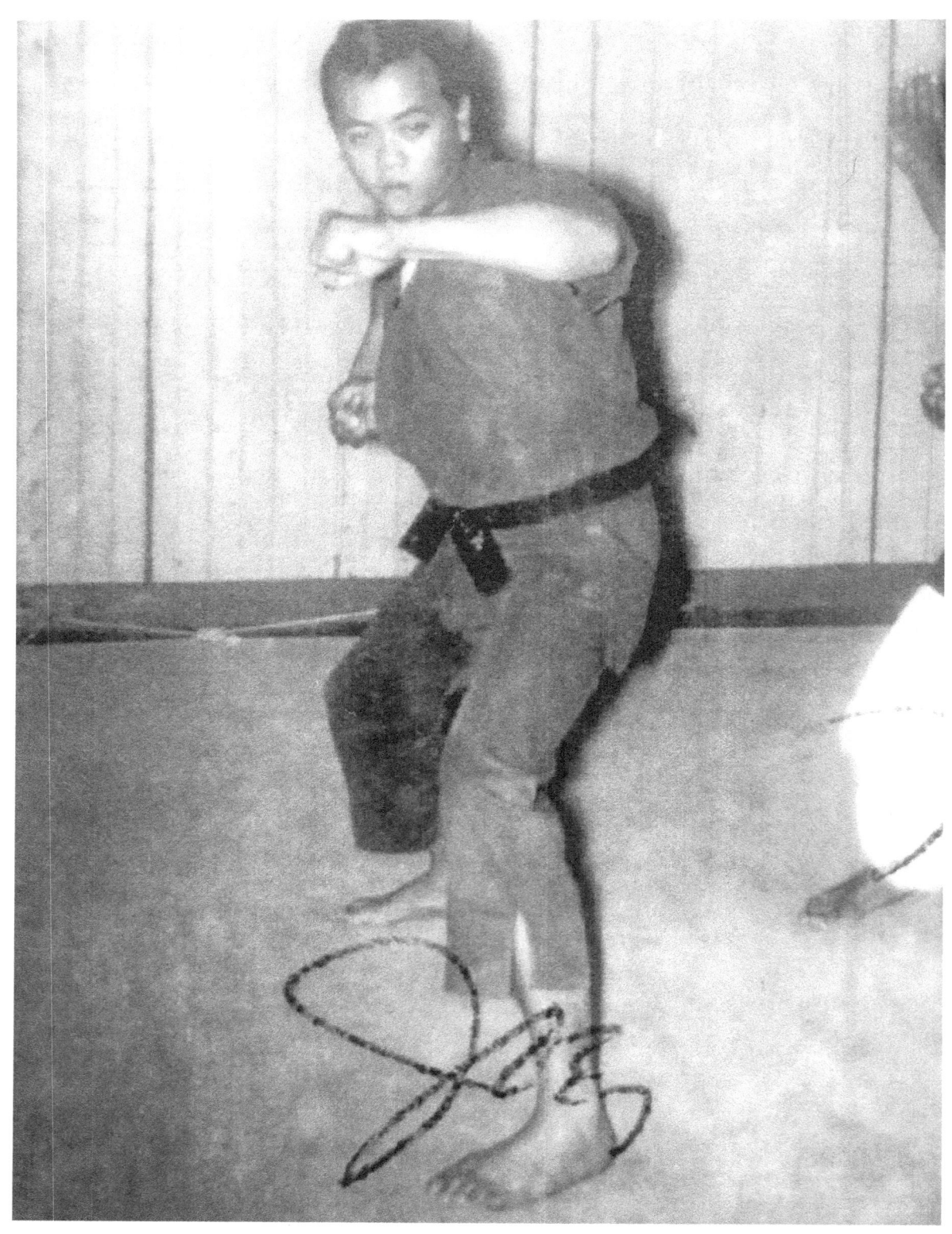

"Professor" Joe Emperado

Joe is pictured at left.

Joe pictured rear right.

Always remember me. Surrounding Joe's casket above are Sijo Adriano (with hand on his brother Joe), Marino Tiwinak, Frank Ordonez and Professor Chow. Standing behind Professor Chow is Abraham "Bruddah Abe" Kamahoahoa. Godin is standing third over Sijo's left shoulder.

Joe Emperado's pallbearers. Walter Godin left middle. Sid Asuncion far right.

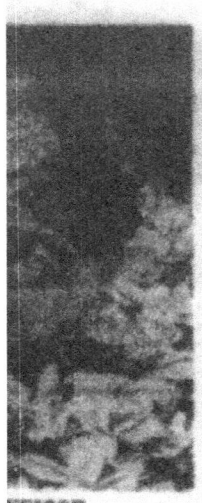

Mrs. Corey Decides Board Is Man's World

Former schoolmarm Lillian H. Corey sadly refurled her crusading banner yesterday and announced that the cry for a "woman's touch" at City Hall will not be heard this year.

* * *

SHE CAN'T afford to run for the Board of Supervisors, she said. And since she's not a member of a political party she can't expect any help from the pros.

"The parties don't pay much attention to women," the wife of Oahu Democratic committeeman Ralph E. Corey told reporters.

* * *

MRS. COREY said last December that she would run for the Board because "These men are too slow, too reactionary, too conservative."

She felt "a woman's touch is necessary... A woman isn't as vacillating as a man."

Fidel Beligan

Graveside services with full military honors will be held at the National Memorial Cemetery of the Pacific at 10 a.m. tomorrow for Fidel J. Beligan, 49, who died May 18 at Tripler Army Hospital.

Mr. Beligan, who lived at 1065 Aala St., was employed at the Rattan Art Gallery. He was born Aug. 5, 1906, in Santa Cruz, Philippine Islands. He is survived by a brother there.

Friends may call from 6 to 9

Obituaries

Emperado Rites On Wednesday

Funeral services will be held at 9 a.m. Wednesday at St. Theresa's Catholic Church for Joseph Directo Emperado, 28, who died Friday evening at St. Francis Hospital.

* * *

MR. EMPERADO was born June 29, 1928, and had resided in Honolulu all his life. He lived with his family at 1415 Auld Ln.

He is survived by a daughter, Jodi Emperado; his father, Juan Emperado; his mother, Mrs. Severina D. Bridges; two brothers, Larry Ramos, of Chicago, Ill., and Adriano Emperado, and three sisters, Mrs. Earl (Betty) Smith of Bremerton, Wash., Mrs. Manuel (Connie) Marcello Sr. of Honolulu and Mrs. Eugenio (Ella) Banaga of Hilo, Hawaii.

* * *

MR. EMPERADO was assistant chief instructor of the Palama Settlement Kajukenbo self-defense club, a member of the Hawaiian Pineapple Co. bowling league and the ILWU.

Friends may call at the family home after 7 p.m. Tuesday and from 7 a.m. until the time of services Wednesday. Burial will be at Nuuanu Memorial Park.

Joe's obituary in the local newspaper.

Case H-29234

Evidence recovered from the victim: One pair of Judo pants, black in color, attach tie cord on either side. One t-shirt, red in color, sleeveless. One pair of leather slippers, cross-over type.

Evidence recovered from suspect: a 2 1/2 inch long double-bladed knife. 1 millimeter wide. Yellow plastic handle. "Hallowed Ground" is imprinted on the handle. The shorter blade is 1 1/2 inch long, and the tip is chipped off, and is 1/4 inch wide. The handle is 3 inches long and 1/2 inch wide.

Synopsis: Victim Joseph Emperado was involved in a fight with the named suspects and suffered multiple stab wounds from a sharp instrument. He drove home from the scene, was later transported to St. Francis hospital by C&C ambulance, and was admitted to surgery for treatment where he subsequently expired at 10:25 am 5-30-58 as a result of his wounds.

Cause of death: At 9:35 am 5-31-58 Saturday they logged the record book at C&C morgue for the cause of death one: Joseph Emperado, age 28, 1415 Alud Ln. Filipino male, mechanic helper Hawaiian Pineapple Company: Hemorrhage laceration of the left intercostal artery due to stab wound.

Autopsy performed by Dr. A. Majosaka 7:15 am 5-31-58 ID established 11:40 am 5-30-58, identified by mother, one Severina Emperado, 55 years.

Murder scene: Sidewalk fronting 367 N. Beretania St. Pink Elephant Bar. At approximately 2:15 am Friday 5-30-58. Victim was taken to St. Francis hospital (Liliha St). Admitted at 4:10 am 5-30-58 with multiple stab wounds on his back, chest, and both arms.

Treatment: X-Ray of the chest and suturing of wounds are recommended. Treated by Intern Y.S Chun - Disposition: confined for treatment.

Time of death: 10:25 am 5-30-58 Friday - Pronounced dead by Dr. Edmond Lee.

Coroner arrival: 11:25 am Maurice Lee 5-30-58. Removed body noon 5-30-58

Suspects:
1) Thomas Masato Miura
Occupation: unemployed age 23: arrested 5-30-58 7:00 pm.
Assault and battery with a weapon Misdemeanor 1.
Arresting Officer H. Burns, badge #277

2) William Sagolili
Occupation: Laborer at McKee-Nordic-Meyer age 21.
(It's not clear who the arresting officer was or the time.)
Assault and battery with a weapon. Misdemeanor 1. He was friends with Shimabuku.

3) George Yutaka Shimabuku
Occupation: Mason age 22: arresting Officer Francis Sakai badge #295.
Arrested at 5-30-58, 7:30 pm. at 825 Kaiama Rd.
Charge: Murder felony 1

Victim: Joe Emperado, age 28 (DOB June 29, 1929), employed by

Hawaiian Pineapple Company. Occupation: Mechanic helper. Place of residence: 1415 Alud Lane #2

Witness: Walter L.N. Godin age 21, Employed by Hawaiian Steel and Reinforcement Co. Occupation: Laborer.

Witness: Rose Sabat age 31: Employed by Pink Elephant Bar
Occupation: Waitress
Living as common-law wife to victim Joe Emperado, 1.5 years.

Witness: Elizabeth Tabag age 21
Occupation: Waitress Pink Elephant Bar

Witness: Charles (Charlie) Takara age 35
Occupation: Owner of Pink Elephant Bar

Witness: Bernice Tong age: 30 unemployed

Witness: Rosalie (Rosie) Tapac age 42
Occupation: Owner of Rosario Cafe

Witness: Phillipe Flores age 45
Occupation: Handyman at Pink Elephant bar

Statements from suspects during interrogations:
Note: During the interrogations, Miura-Shimabuku and Sagolili refer to Godin as the "potagee guy" (Hawaiian dialect for Portuguese), and refer

to Emperado as the "pake guy." (Chinese Hawaiian dialect).

William Sagolili- IR#5-8:55 pm 5-30-58 8:55 pm.

Police reporter: James Sakai - Shorthand

Detective Leonard Gunderson and Detective Abraham Aiona.

"Went into the bar about 1:15 am. We had gone to another bar (unknown) in Chinatown before Pink Elephant and had some drinks there. Drove to Pink Elephant by Shimabuku's 1951 or '52 Chevy 4-door white color sedan. Parked the car on Hall Street. Sat down and had Lucky Lager beers. Elizabeth (waitress) came and sat by us and talked to us (Sagolili and Elizabeth were classmates). The Potagee guy and Shimabuku kept staring at each other. The Potagee comes to the table and tells Shimabuku, "What are you looking at?" Shimabuku says back "What are you looking at me for?" Godin tells them "We go outside and take me in your car anywhere and I fight all three of you there!". Shimabuku didn't say anything. Was getting close to closing time and the workers were putting up the chairs. I asked Elizabeth if we could finish our beers. She said ok. So we downed our beers. George remarked that if they throw us out he was going to lick everyone in the bar. At about 2:00 am. Shimabuku yelled out "I wipe out anybody here!" The Potagee then came up to Shimabuku and asked Shimabuku if he wanted to fight-fight now! Shimabuku said he didn't want to fight. The Chinese guy (Emperado) came over and asked what the matter was and made them shake hands. On our way out Godin and Shimabuku eyed each other up and Godin said, "One of these days you going to get lickins the way you act." Shimabuku said "I no care." They go outside. They started to argue. Godin punches Shimabuku in the mouth Shimabuku flew against a car that was parked in the front. All of a sudden the guy that died came from the bar doorway and charged George and

George flew against the back bumper of the car. Then Godin punched me in the face when I tried to break up the scuffle between Joe and Shimabuku so I went after Godin. Godin got me in a headlock. Then I heard someone say "someone got cut!" I yelled to Miura to get Godin off of me. Miura went after Godin. Godin released me and then kicked me in the face. (Sagolili points to his upper lip to show where Godin kicked him). Then the Potagee challenges all three of us. So we all charged after him and ran across the street. But we changed our minds and ran to Shimabuku's car. When we got in the car I notice George didn't have his shirt on. It must have gotten torn off during the fight. Then George told us that he stabbed the Pake guy. Shimabuku then showed us the knife and it had blood on the blade. I tell him you should have not poked him because if he dies they gonna come after me first. After all, I went to school with Elizabeth the waitress who sat with us. Shimabuku said "I don't give a shit if that bastard dies or not!" Shimabuku also told us when we were walking out of the Pink Elephant he already had his left hand in his left pocket and that he was holding the knife blade open and that he was going to cut up the first guy who punched him. Shimabuku is the type of guy that brags. All of us guys call him punchy. And he thinks he can lick anybody. In the car, he told us he kills anybody who fools with him. We went to my house in Lanakila housing to get Shimabuku a shirt. Then we went to Kapiolani drive inn to eat breakfast. Then went to Kau Kau corner for coffee. Then went to the house of William Hayno. We got there around five am. And slept till seven am. Went to William's brother's house in Waipahu at nine thirty am. And went back to town at five thirty pm. At seven pm when I got home my dad and sister told me that Emperado died. Later I called Miura and told him."

Thomas Miura Statement 9:35 pm, 5-30-58, IR#5

(Detective Leonard Gunderson and Detective Abraham Aiona. Police reporter James Sakai – shorthand.)

"Came into bar about 1:00 AM. We sat at the table and ordered beers. Shimabuku and Potagee guy eyed each other up. Potagee came to the table and ask Shimabuku "What are you staring at me for?" Shimabuku answers back the same thing. Potagee guy tells us to take him in our car and drive him anywhere and he fights all three of us. Then he walks away. Shimabuku later said he take on anyone. Godin came over and asked him to go outside. The Pake guy comes over and makes them shake hands. After closing, Godin and Shimabuku argued outside. Godin punches Shimabuku in the mouth. Shimabuku flew against a car that was parked in the front and then fell to the sidewalk at which Joe went for Shimabuku. The fight went against the wall of the building. Then I heard Joe say "I got sliced" at that time I went to go help Sagolili who was fighting with Godin. I struck Godin twice. Godin punched me three times in the face and kicked my right leg. Then we chased Godin across Beretania Street for a short distance and then jump into Shimabuku's car and drove off. Shimabuku was the driver me and Sagolili sat in the back. I noticed Shimabuku was not wearing his shirt. Must have gotten torn off during the struggle. We headed to Lanakila housing to get Shimabuku a shirt. During the ride home. Shimabuku told us he had stabbed the Pake guy who was Joe, several times. He also showed us the knife which he had used. Sagolili told him you shouldn't have stabbed him. Shimabuku says, "I don't give a shit if the guy dies!" Shimabuku told us when we were leaving the Pink Elephant he already had his left hand in his left pocket and had the blade opened. And he was going to stab the first guy who hit him. I did not see Shimabuku stab Emperado but I noticed Joe was bleeding from his right arm."

Rose Sabat statement 2:55 pm, 5-30-58.
(Detective Gunderson interviewer. Two interviews were conducted, one at Saint Francis, and one at HPD.)

"At about 10:30 pm 5-29-58, Joe and Walter came into the bar and sat at a table near the bar. She was tending the bar at the time. She states that Godin and Joe were both sober at the time. Just before midnight, she saw them change tables and sit with the owner of the bar Charlie Takara. Just before closing time, she saw Godin walk to the table where Elizabeth and the three males were sitting and heard Godin say "What are you looking at me for?" She heard Godin and Shimabuku arguing, then saw Joe go over to the table and break it up. And made them shake hands. Godin went back to his table. At closing time, Joe walked to the bar to talk to Charlie. She did not see Joe leave she was busy cleaning up at the time. She heard Elizabeth yelling from the doorway. "Uncle Joe fighting!" She rushed to the sidewalk and saw Joe and Shimabuku fighting. She pulled Joe away. Then Joe asked her how he got blood on his arm. She also noticed he was bleeding from his right arm. She then took him to Rosario Cafe next door to the Pink Elephant where he washed up, while Walter Godin was fighting the other three males and then ran. She added she wasn't sure if they caught up to him or not. About this time a motorcycle officer arrived and she told him that Joe had been cut with a knife. Joe told the officer he did not want to do anything and the officer left the scene shortly thereafter. Joe took Rose into his car and drove home. When they got home Joe lay down on the bed and complained of having difficulty breathing. She checked his body and found he had been stabbed in his back and his chest. She then called the ambulance although he did not want her to do so. He was then taken to Saint Francis hospital for further treatment."

Statement: Elizabeth Tabag, 9:08 am, 5-30-58
(Interviewed by Sgt. Abraham Aiona Badge #104)

"Knows William Sagolili. They were classmates. She went and sat in her car outside the bar after her shift was over at midnight. Went back into the bar at 12:30 am to play shuffleboard machine. A few minutes later she saw Sagolili and the two other males and sat with them. She said later Walter came to the table and told Shimabuku "What are you staring at me for?" Shimabuku said back the same. Joe came over and made them shake hands. She saw Joe later strike Shimabuku both of them fell against a parked car. While the two were fighting Rose came out and pulled Joe away to stop fighting. She also said she saw Godin fighting with Sagolili and Miura. Also stated that the three men came into the bar prior on Sunday 5-25-58 with three other males with them. Also stated she did not see anyone with a weapon."

Statement: Rosalie Tapac, 2:00 pm, 5-31-58
(Detective L. Gunderson)

"At 2:10 am she was closing up her business when she heard some commotion going on outside her cafe on the sidewalk where she saw Joe and Walter fighting. She saw Joe a short distance away from Godin fighting a Japanese boy and pushing away Rose Sabat who was trying to stop the fight. She heard Joe say "Who poke me with the knife." Then Rose brought Joe into her business to wash up. Where Rosalie noticed he was cut on his back and bleeding. She also noticed he was bleeding from a wound on his right arm and stomach area. Then she said later Rose and Joe got into Joe's car and drove off. She stated at no time did she see anyone with a knife. Further added that she would not be able to identify the men involved with the fight if she saw them again."

Statement: Bernice Tong
(Detective L. Gunderson 5-31-58)

"Stated she saw Godin and the boy with bangs in his hair like a girl get into an argument. Then Joe broke it up and made them shake hands. She didn't see anyone leave at closing time because she went into the lady's room. But she heard a commotion outside and saw Walter Godin and another boy squaring off and fist-fighting. Not wanting to be involved she walked away and went to the Rainbow Fountain to get something to eat. Stated she did not witness the fight with Joe and Shimabuku and did not see anyone with a knife."

Statement: Phillipe Flores, 12:05 pm, 5-31-58
(Detective L. Gunderson)

"Did not see anything. He was busy in the back filling the icebox up with beer. Heard some commotion. When he went out to look and saw Joe standing on the sidewalk bleeding from some kind of wound on his right arm. He figured the fight was all over and went back inside to fill the icebox."

Statement: Charles Takara, 4:15 pm, 5-30-58

(Detective L. Gunderson)

"Stated at about 12:30 am 5-30-58. Three young men came into his place of business and sat down at a table near the jukebox and men's toilet. Him Bernice Tong, Walter Godin, and Joe Emperado were sitting at about three tables away from the three young men. Joe was in a good frame of mind and was massaging his (Charlie's) neck and talking and laughing. The three young men were drinking Lucky Luck lager beers and were sitting with an off-duty waitress Elizabeth Tapac. At about 1:45 am, he left his table and went to the men's room. While in the men's room he heard a commotion going on outside. He came out to check. He thought Elizabeth and Bernice were the cause of the commotion so he scolded Bernice. She had told him she was not at fault. He then went out to the sidewalk and saw Joe and the boy with hair combed with bangs down his forehead. Both men were on the ground on the sidewalk. They both got up and noticed Joe was bleeding from a wound on his right arm. At this time Rose was holding his arm. Joe was taken into Rosaria Cafe with Rose. Shortly thereafter he saw Joe leaving. Rosaria Cafe, driving off in his car. Joe was the driver. He further stated the commotion started when he was in the men's room, so he didn't see how the fight started and did not see anyone with a knife or witness the stabbing."

Statement: Walter L.N. Godin

(Detective L. Gunderson, Badge #169)

"I had gone to the bar about 9:30-10:00 pm. I sat at a table with Joe who was already there and Charlie Takara and Bernice. At about 1:30 three young boys entered the establishment. They sat at a table near the jukebox and men's room. While I was drinking my beer and looking up I saw this guy eyeing me up. At the time I didn't bother. I went again for my glass and started drinking. I looked up and he was still eyeing me up, with his head like a boxer going back and forth and making stabbing motions with his hand. So I continued drinking and when it was almost closing time, he passed a remark to me. He said, "I hope that guy comes to the table." At first, I hold back my temper. Then he said it a second time. "I hope that guy comes to the table." So I stood up and told him "Hey bull you looking for trouble, if you like me and you go!" And he started getting sassy and cocky. Then Joe went to the table and talked to them. He finally calms the guy down to shake hands with me. Then I left. Joe calls me over to the table and tells me to shake hands with the guys. But I didn't want to. He called me again and I went over to the table. I shook the guy's hand and remarked that we guys are local and we got to stick together. So I went back to my table. But since the bar was already supposed to close, I went over to the bar and waited for Joe to come out. While I was at the bar the three guys walked over to me. So on their way out, I guess they were waiting for me. Because a few minutes later I went out and the three of them were on my left side. So I looked over at them and the guy that did the slaying started Bobbing his head back and forth and was mumbling to himself. Then he said "What you think you rugged? Huh, Potagee?!!" So I told him if he wanted to beef why doesn't he come to my car or I go in theirs and take me anywhere and I fight all you guys. So we started to brawl and Joe comes out to stop the fight. He grabbed that guy and went in between two cars. They probably fell because I couldn't see them. Then the Filipino boy went to help George so I struck him. When I struck him he was jumping around and calling me a punk. Then the two guys came after me. So I stand in a Kempo Karate position and one of the guys says forget it don't go near the guy. But I guess he was really angry and he came charging me. I got him into a headlock. When I had him in a headlock his other friend came after me. I kicked him in the leg. I finally released the headlock on the guy and went over to help Joe. I intended to go back to back with him and we can fight off these guys. Then Joe said, "These punks stabbed me!" So the next thing on my mind was to get these guys away from Joe. Joe chargers the guy that went stab him, But I saw he had no power to do what he was trying to do. So I swore at them. Told them to come to get me. I suck them over to me. Get their attention on me not Joe. So I challenge all three of them. So they came after me. They chase me I started to pick up speed. Then I spun and turned by the bakery and they were gone. I came back to the scene and everything was quiet down already. I didn't know where the three guys went to. Finding the place was empty I went to Joe's house. I found him on the bed lying there. And his exact words to me were, "Don't worry Godin, we get the guys."

The detective asks Godin once more some questions about the time Joe and he came in, which is about the same as Rose's statement. Also, the time the three males came into the bar was about the same. Forthcoming questions are important.

Detective: *Was there anything peculiar about any of these three boys?*
Godin: *Yeah I watched them come in they looked very cocky.*
D: *Was there anything in their appearance?*
G: *Appearance was pretty tough looking.*
D: *How many boys were actually in the fight with Joe?*

G: *Just the one who did the slaying.*

D: *Did the other two have a chance to fight with Joe?*

G: *I kept them from going to him.*

D: *Would you recognize the boy who fought with Joe if you saw him?*

G: *Yes sir.*

D: *Did you see anyone with a knife?*

G: *No sir.*

D: *Who was bleeding?*

G: *Joe.*

D: *Where?*

G: *On his side. Not sure if back or front.*

D: *Did Joe say anything?*

G: *Just told Rose to let him go because he was going to get the guy who stabbed him.*

D: *Did he indicate that he knew who stabbed him?*

G: *No, but he went right to the guy he was fighting with.*

D: *What did that boy look like?*

G: *Well he combed his hair down like a girl with bangs, mean-looking. He looked pretty crazy to me, punchy.*

D: *Did these three boys appear to be under the influence of liquor?*

G: *Yes sir.*

D: *Would you say they were drunk?*

G: *No sir just acting.*

D: *What was your condition?*

G: *I wasn't drunk.*

D: *What was Joe's condition?*

G: *He wasn't drunk either.*

Detective Gunderson leaves the room and returns with George Shimabuku and asks Godin if he recognizes him. Godin says yes and the detective asks if he knows his name. Godin tells him no. The detective tells him George Shimabuku. The detective returns again and again with the other two suspects and asks the same questions. Godin answers the same that he recognizes them but does not know their names again the detective gives him their names. Note: (I believe that was how old police work was done during that period.) Godin makes one final statement to Detective Gunderson. He tells the detective again that while Shimabuku was outside the Pink Elephant bar on the sidewalk Shimabuku looked over at him and kept making poking motions with his hand like he wanted to stab him. Statements concluded at 11:06 am, 5-31-58

Supplement report: At 5:35 pm 5-30-58 Officer Sasaki #295, beat 37 3rd watch, received information from dispatcher officer Tommy Farr to check 825 Kaiama Rd and be on the lookout for one George Shimabuku who is a prime suspect for murder. The suspect arrived at his home at 7:30 pm 5-30-58, at which time he was placed under arrest. Found the murder weapon in his right front pocket while being searched, which he stated to Officer Sasaki. "This is the knife." The suspect was arrested and booked for murder. The knife was seized for evidence.

Statement: George Shimabuku
(Detective Leonard Gunderson #169, 5-30-58 I/R#1, 8:10 pm - 8:30 pm)
"Shimabuku claimed Joe hit him in the mouth knocking him down on the sidewalk. He got up. Pulled the knife out of his pocket which he held in his left hand and started to poke Joe with the knife. Also stated that he

could use either hand very well. Could not recall how many times he stabbed Joe. Or where he had poked him. But saw blood coming out of Joe's arm Joe did not fall but Joe did not attack him anymore either. Since he didn't attack anymore he put the knife back. Stuck it in the same left pocket trouser."

Attorney arrives for Shimabuku at 8:45 am 5-31-58.

Attorney M. Symonds at the detective bureau talked with Shimabuku in I/R #1. After he was through talking with his client, he left. After speaking with his attorney, George refuses to give any more statements.

Shimabuku identified 8:50 am 5-31-58 by Elizabeth Tabag.

Elizabeth Tabag looked into I/R#1 where Shimabuku was conferring with his attorney. She then stated that he was the boy she had seen fighting with Joe. At the time Attorney Elton Sakamoto was also talking to Shimabuku. Knife identified by Sagolili and Miura. At the time each suspect was questioned. Each identified the knife that Shimabuku showed to them as a weapon. Both said it looked like the weapon.

Sagolili and Miura were discharged at 11:40 am. 5-31-58.

Two of the three men, William Sagolili, 21, and Thomas Miura, 23, were discharged from custody as they were not involved in the fatal stabbing of the victim. George Yutaka (it was misspelled *Yutaka*) Shimabuku, the defendant, age 22, was charged with murder in the second degree (section 291-1 RL/55) on Saturday 5-31-58 at 1:30 pm. He was taken to receiving desk by Detective Abraham Aiona and turned over to the desk Lieutenant.

Follow-up information: At approximately 4:15 pm on 5-30-58, a check-up was made to arrest William Sagolili, as he was the only known suspect at that time. His sister was home but did not want to give her name, but gave information on her brother. Sagolili's sister related she got a call from William Hayno's wife about the fight all three got into the previous night. Sagolili's sister informed officer Raymond Kawano (beat 21, 3rd watch) that she most likely suspected George Shimabuku because he has an uncontrollable temper.

Professor Godin told me that the judge dismissed the case, stating because he and Joe were martial artists, George and the others were protecting themselves.

On July 10, 1958, George Yutaka Shimabuku was indicted for the murder of Joe Emperado in the 2nd degree.

On July 11th, 1958 a plea of not guilty was entered.

On August 11th, 1958 he changed the plea to guilty of manslaughter.

On August 25th, 1958 he was sentenced to 10 years in prison. The majority of the sentence was suspended and he was placed on probation for five years. Probation was given on Tuesday, September 9th, 1958 at 10:17 am by Judge Albert M. Felix III.

Professor Godin's main objective was to one day tell the story of his experiences with Joe and of Joe's incredible martial arts skills. He described Joe as having incredible flowing power, similar to an approaching storm. He was a unique and gifted martial artist, who had new ideas for Kajukenbo. Godin told me in his interview that he and Joe would often go to secluded parks and train in self-defense techniques. Techniques that they would not practice in class. And that one day he wanted to go on his own and take Godin with him.

Godin also wanted to let the Kajukenbo world know that not just any punk could have taken out Joe, it took a high caliber of evil to do that. A man who had no regard for anyone and no remorse for anything he did. A killer of that magnitude. One George Shimabuku.

His friend, William Sagolili told the detectives, "George told us that he thinks he can lick everybody and that he kills anyone who fools with him." Shimabuku, while out on probation for Joe's murder, would commit another murder in 1963 that was reduced to manslaughter. He then murdered another person while out on probation in August 1967. For that murder, he would be sentenced to life. He then received a second life sentence on July 29th, 1968 for killing inmate Ben Aipa (not the famous surfer).

Hawaii became a safer place when George Shimabuku was taken off the streets for good. All the facts prove that Shimabuku was a bad seed. George looked for trouble but needed a weapon when someone stood up to him. To me, that is evil and cowardice.

I asked Professor Godin while he was incarcerated if he saw Shimabuku. He told me that they sent Shimabuku to a prison on the mainland. He said to me, *"If he was in population with me, either he would be dead or I would be dead!"*

My objective as to writing this chapter was to exonerate my instructor from the Kajukenbo world and also to let an important piece of Kajukenbo history be told as it was. There are too many people who claim to know what happened that night who were told second-hand stories, bits, and pieces that were told by others in the Kajukenbo system at that time, and judged my instructor by those accusations.

No one could have known what happened unless they were there or asked the people who were there at the time.

Professor Godin would go on to be Professor Adriano Emperado's bodyguard when traveling. If he thought Godin was a coward, why would he have Godin protect him?

Godin told me in the years after the incident that he stayed with the Emperado system. Not once did Adriano ask him to tell him what happened that night. Not a single time. Professor Adriano never brought up the subject. He told me that Emperado was the kind of guy who if he didn't bring up a subject, you don't talk about it or bring it up. But still, Godin found it strange that he never questioned him on the issue of the death of his brother. Professor Adriano, for reasons known only to him, didn't bring up that issue.

This brings me to the myths that were repeated for nearly 60 years. The first is that *Kajukenbo black belts were in the bar hours before the murder*, allegedly drinking and talking with Joe and Walter, and also that *if they had stayed, Joe would still be alive today.*

If that were the case, Rose Sabat would have mentioned it in her statement. According to her, Joe and Walter came into the bar at 10:30 pm and sat with Charlie Takara, the owner of the bar. No one else came in with them and sat with them. Rose knew the Kajukenbo black belts well, for she was Joe's common-law wife for a year and a half.

Another myth is that *Joe walked home after being stabbed*. Joe lived 0.9 miles from the bar, but according to the above witness statements, he drove home with Rose.

Godin ran away when the knife was pulled. That's the statement that frustrated me the most. People tagged my instructor as a coward when the chips were down.

In 1987, Panther Productions made a video on the history, concepts, and philosophy of Kajukenbo. In one segment of the tape, it was discussed how Joe was killed and it was stated that "after Joe was stabbed, Godin ran away and left Joe." From that point forward, many Kajukenbo students perceived Godin to be a coward who left Joe to die. Godin carried that cross for many years up until his death.

I can't say enough but to read William Sagolili's statement about how Godin challenged all three of them, and then read my instructor's statement as to why he did and read all the witness's statements stating that at no time did anyone see a weapon. Even Joe didn't realize that he had been stabbed and sliced at the time.

Godin ran to get help.

One Kempo black belt told me that he heard from his instructor that Godin confided in him, stating he ran to get help. Godin, in his statement, was trying to lure all three men away from Joe because he saw that Joe was not capable of being able to defend himself. So he challenged all three men as he claimed in his statement, which corroborated with what Sagolili stated previously. Furthermore, he stopped and turned around to continue to fight the three assailants when he reached the bakery. Was he looking for the baker to help him?

Godin told me he was tagged as an outcast in the Kajukenbo system and most of the higher ranks felt it was his fault that Joe was killed. No one wanted to associate with him after the incident. No higher ranks wanted to talk to him. He told me that when he went to visit Joe in the hospital all the black belts were there and all stared him down. Joe had already passed away when he came to visit. He got the same treatment at the funeral. So how could he have talked with anyone when no one wanted to talk with him? The same fact goes with Professor Adriano, he never asked Godin about the incident.

There are many more stories that I can talk about, and probably a lot that I've never heard of, but I believe that I have made my point and shown you all of the true evidence that has been presented.

It's been nearly 60 years since Professor Joe passed, and 16 years have passed since my instructor has been gone. Now they are training together once again. Joe left us in 1958. Godin left us in 2001. They waited 43 years to train together once again.

What became of Thomas Miura and William Sagolili is unknown. George Shimabuku at age 81 is currently serving his double life sentence in an Arizona state prison. He refused an interview with me in 2002.

U.S. Department of Justice

Federal Bureau of Prisons

United States Penitentiary, Florence

Warden's Office
P.O. Box 7500
Florence, CO 81226-7500

June 12, 2002

Mr. David Tavares
Fighting Arts Hawaii
PMB 208, 590 Farrington Highway, #210
Kapolei, HI 96707

RE: **Interview Request - SHIMABUKU, George**
Register Number: 01784-135

Dear Mr. Tavares:

I wish to inform you that your request to interview inmate George Shimabuku has been reviewed and processed. Unfortunately, we are unable to permit this interview to occur. Mr. Shimabuku has declined to be interviewed at this time.

I trust that this information is helpful.

Respectfully,

J. E. Gunja, Warden
USP Florence, Colorado

cc   Media File
       Central File

FOUR IN THE SHADOWS

"Those whose light burn within, need not the spotlight."
-Unknown

George Chang
1925-2003

Born George Chen Yoke Chang, on July 12th, 1925 in Honolulu, Hawaii. Of all the five founders in Kajukenbo history, Professor George is the only name that has been recorded incorrectly throughout the years. For a reason that is not known, his name was mistakenly identified as Clarence.

Professor Chang is credited for incorporating Chinese Boxing into Kajukenbo. Contrary to Kajukenbo history, it is recorded that at age 12 he traveled to his father's homeland of Kwangtung, China, and studied Sil Lum Kung Fu, but according to Chang's last living sibling (his sister), that statement is incorrect. He never traveled back to his father's homeland, but rather stayed in Hawaiian territories in his adolescent age.

George began his Kung Fu training at age 16 under the feared Wong Kok Fut in Kalihi. Wong who taught out of his garage trained and taught a unique blend of Kung Fu from his native tribe the Hakka in Southern China, a gypsy style of Chinese boxing, as the established Kung Fu community referred to it for the fact that the Hakka tribe were populated by gypsies. Sifu Wong's system consisted of only seven hand tricks and one form. How much of Sifu Wong's hand strikes, blocks, and kata were influenced in Kajukenbo are uncertain, but most Hawaii Kung Fu stylists agree that Wong had exceptional hand speed and generated incredible power in his long and short-range strikes, a strong attribute that most if not all Kajukenbo artist possess.

In 1950, at age 25, a young George would see combat during the Korean conflict as a U.S. Marine. It would later be rumored that he was killed in action. How the rumor came to be is unclear. One possibility could have been that George was not in contact with anyone when he returned. It would be at Peter Choo's funeral services in 1997 when he came to give his final respects to his friend and co-founder brother where the rumor was proven to be untrue.

George was regarded as the most private and remote of the five founders. There are no known existing photos that have all five founders together. Chang's photo is always cropped into the photos of the other four founders who are seated together.

Professor Chang left for his military duty while Kajukenbo was still in its grassroots stage, and he mysteriously separated himself from the Kajukenbo system when he returned home from the war to live a quiet life and retired from a city and county of Honolulu position he held with the Board of Water Supply on Oahu.

He passed away on January 15th, 2003 in Honolulu, Hawaii.

Frank Ordonez
(1927-Present)

Born Frank Ferino Ordonez, February 15th, 1927 in Puunene, Maui. Frank's father moved the Ordonez family to Oahu when he was still in grade school. He began his martial arts journey at the tender age of 14. Studied under Sam Luke Sr., a Danzan Ryu Instructor who trained under Professor Okazaki. It was at his Dan Zan Ryu training where he would meet Joe Holck.

He enlisted in the U.S. Army at age 18. He was stationed at Ft. Shafter, and served in the Signal Corps, Unit 8309, under Captain William Hoover. It would be at Shafter where he would launch his amateur boxing career.

Frank fought on the Army boxing team as a Bantamweight and was trained by highly regarded boxing coach Tommy Toyama. He was a member of Toyama's boxing team that would bring home the silver medal in the territories boxing team championships in 1946. He befriended fellow boxing team member welterweight Peter Choo and later convinced Choo to cross-train with him and Holck in Ju-Jitsu under Sam Luke Sr., and Kempo-Ju-Jitsu with Thomas Young.

Professor Frank is primarily responsible for bringing together the other four founders to train together and express their ideas to incorporate each artist's style to create the world's first mixed martial art. Training from 1947 thru 1949 in an abandoned barracks across his Halawa housing home, Ordonez would schedule training sessions with childhood friend and well-known Kempo stylist, Adriano Emperado, Ju-Jitsu training partner Joe Holck, and fellow boxer Peter Choo, who brought his friend George

Chang. At first, training on a regular basis, to experience each other's styles and exchange ideas, then trial and error of fighting techniques, then hone and perfect the new techniques.

Ordonez was the driving force in pioneering Kajukenbo and was partly responsible (but not credited) for giving the newly born art its name. He would go on to help the Emperado brothers with the teachings at three Kajukenbo schools, Palama, Kaimuki, and Wahiawa.

In 1958, he wrote the Kajukenbo prayer while doing government contract work and while teaching Kajukenbo on Wake Island. A devoted Catholic and former altar boy, young Frank felt the need to write the prayer, because in his heart he felt that the art he and his friends created was a gift from God, for the protection of one's self, family, and country. It would take the young Co-founder six months to write the prayer. Feeling it necessary to make the prayer correct in sequence in its reciting as spirit first, mind second, body third. Upon his return to Oahu, he had the prayer blessed by a priest at his parish at St. Joseph's church in Waipahu.

Having the vision to combine the fighting arts proved Ordonez to be light years ahead of his time in martial arts philosophy, and having the wisdom to give the glory back to the almighty is an example that showed the spiritual level of the martial arts that he achieved, a characteristic few martial artists reaches in their lifetime or neglect to strive for.

He worked at Hawaiian Tel for 25 years and retired in 1985.

Frank is the last living legend of the five founders and he celebrated his 90th birthday in February 2017, and is still speaking at seminars and making appearances with his Ordonez Kajukenbo Ohana organization.

Peter Choo
(1926-1997)

Born Peter Young Yil Choo, August 21st, 1926 in Honolulu, Hawaii. Professor Choo's base in martial arts was from his father as a youth learning backyard Korean martial arts. He trained in biddy boxing and won the Joe Lynch boxing award in 1937 at age 11.

Peter enlisted in the U.S. Army in 1944 and trained on the Army boxing team where he met Frank Ordonez. Professor Choo fought as a welterweight and held the All-Army welterweight crown. He was considered by Ordonez as a natural in the fighting arts, always excelling with every art he learned throughout his military career, traveling to different countries, and learning each native land's art. He saw combat during the Korean conflict and had been temporarily based there after the conflict ended. While in Korea, he refined his father's art that was taught to him as a child by training with the legendary Jhoon Rhee. In 1955 transferred to Japan and studied Aikido training both with Morehei Uyeshiba and Koichi Tohei. Later he transferred to Okinawa and trained in Shorinji Karate under Ed Takai. He went on to continue his boxing training with his European military tours, winning multiple titles in his division.

Peter Choo exemplified the martial arts spirit, endlessly filling his martial arts cup of knowledge by absorbing all martial arts when the opportunity came. The true illustration of what the Kajukenbo philosophy is based upon. A man who was a co-founder of a new hybrid art, but still had the burning desire to learn more from others and add to his arsenal.

He retired from the U.S. Army in 1965 as a Command Sergeant Major E-9, the highest level an enlisted soldier can attain, proving Professor

Choo always strived to reach the highest levels in his martial arts training and life. He passed away on June 9th, 1997 in Honolulu, Hawaii.

Joe Holck
(1927-2011)

Born Joichi Matsuno, March 28th, 1927, of Japanese-Swedish ancestry. He took the maiden name of his mother, Holck, after the Pearl Harbor attack, due to the anti-Japanese sentiment in the bombing aftermath.

Joe's martial arts studies began in 1938 at age 11. He trained Danzan Ryu Ju-Jitsu under Professor Seishiro Okazaki and later trained under Bing Fai Lau and Siegfried Kufferath. Befriended Frank Ordonez, who was training with Sam Luke Sr. Danzan Ryu at the same time.

Joe enlisted in the United States Army in 1944 at the young age of 17. He became a hand-to-hand combat instructor during basic training due to his martial arts background. At the end of World War II, he was stationed in Germany during the allied occupation. He was assigned to the 9th Infantry division as the hand-to-hand combat instructor for Non Commissioned Officers. He returned to Hawaii in 1947 and reunited his Danzan Ryu training with Sig Kufferath.

In 1948, he started his Judo training under Inouye Sensei in Honolulu and received his Shodan rank two years later.

Joe relocated to Tucson, Arizona in 1964 and he received his 5th degree from the American Ju-Jitsu Institute that same year.

In 1949, after many discussions with Ordonez, he insisted that Kajukenbo should now begin to be taught to the public, but was never credited for it. He was considered the most dedicated to improving the grappling facet of Kajukenbo through his constant training, refining, and elevating in the grappling ranks.

He retired from the Army in 1964 as a full-bird Colonel. In 1967, he founded the School of the Ancient Tradition Black Belt Society, which taught Danzan Ryu, Wado Kai Karate Do, Shorin Ryu Karate, Kajukenbo, and Matsuno Ryu Goshin-Jitsu. According to Frank Ordonez, Holck was considered the brains behind the Kajukenbo pioneering.

Joe Holck passed away on November 6th, 2011 in Tucson, AZ.

Tommy Toyama
(1923-1998)
Kajukenbo's Lost Legacy

Born Thomas Tetsugi Toyama, on July 15, 1923, in Honohina on the Big Island of Hawaii. Toyama and his brother Eisho trained the famous welterweight contender Philip "Wildcat" Kim (43W-15L with 31 KO.)

Toyama was asked by Frank Ordonez to be a part of the Kajukenbo system during the pioneering stages of Kajukenbo, but his commitment to boxing would have been a conflict of interest with the commission. The boxing commission at the time did not want Western boxing connected with the oriental arts as the policy still stands today. Toyama reluctantly turned down the offer. Toyama's western boxing, along with George Chang's Chinese Boxing, would have been a part of the BO in the Kajukenbo name.

Ordonez and Choo would use their boxing skills and conditioning training that was taught to them by Toyama to add to the art arsenal. Toyama did not make the journey with the other five men but played an influential role in two of the five founders, and the fact that he was asked to be a part of Kajukenbo and to add that no other boxer was asked after Toyama, made the need of the mention of his name and write an overview of his story so that we may know a little bit more in-depth about the history of our practicing style and that he will not be forgotten.

Much mahalo for all that you did Tommy, for two of our five founders, and your dedication to the boxing community. Your boxing influence in training Peter Choo and Frank Ordonez by instilling discipline in the training regiment of the fighting arts and helping enhance the punching combination skills and punching power in the Kajukenbo system.

Toyama would pass away on March 26th, 1998, a year after Peter Choo's death. *Aloha Ke Akua*, Tommy Toyama. Goodbye, God bless, a Kajukenbo lost legacy, gone but not forgotten.

Until we meet again.

THE RISING SUN

"Blessed be the lord my rock. Who trains my hands for war, and my fingers for battle."
Psalms: 144-1

Running up Makakilo Drive with my dog Bruce Lee I can see Japan. At the top of the hill, I can see my opponent.

July through September 2008 was the most intense high-level training I ever experienced in my life, harder physically and mentally than training for the 1983 USA/ABF boxing nationals when I was 21. This time I am many years older, and although I'm more focused and more relaxed, there are mixed emotions in my life. My daughter is expecting my first grandchild, a girl. I'm going to be a grandfather at age 47 and I am very happy and excited, but I'm still mourning the loss of my step-dad, Duane Dennison - the man who paid for my martial arts training from age nine until I was 18.

Going to redeem myself, I'm coming off a decision loss in a pankration match against a taller and 35lbs heavier and better ground fighter than me, Maui Kajukenbo stylist, the late Trent Serra, rest in peace. I wanted this fight. This time my opponent is in my weight class, but still, the odds are against me, for my opponent is 26 years my junior, twenty-two-year-old Yasuhiro Shimizu, a wrestling /BJJ fighter.

I'm learning a lot more about BJJ from Danny, Tommy, and my younger competition teammates. All are fighting for Japanese titles.

There are nights I wanted to quit and nights I can't see quitting. I spend a lot of time on my back and am put in the worst positions. I'm taught submission holds and how to escape from them and learn takedowns from Tommy. His older brother Danny, who is also a black belt, is training us with focus mitts, Muay Thai pads, and strength & conditioning training. I realize later he too is training for a grappling match in Japan. I gain much respect for him as an instructor, a martial artist, and a friend, showing dedication to our training before his own.

My teammates are Tommy Lam, Danny Lam, Jeremy Wong, Ryan Scoville, and Keenan Yonimine. Tommy is the Chief Instructor and founder of Kempo Unlimited. He has the Japan experience and has won titles there. He is a very gifted martial artist with exceptional grappling, stand-up fighting, and street self-defense skills. He proved to the fighters in Japan that his method of Kempo was effective. Tommy was the one who asked me if I wanted to fight on the team and go to Japan. Danny Lam is the Head Instructor and Kempo black belt under his brother Tommy, and like Tommy, he is a high-level grappler. Jeremy Wong is a Kempo Unlimited fighter with pankration fighting experience. He is the only fighter that I know that has dropped two of his opponents from what we call in boxing a "shotgun jab." There are two other fighters that I have seen do that; Larry Holmes vs. Ossie Ocasio and Simon Brown vs. Terry Norris. Ryan Scoville is a former Burton Richardson JKD stylist, and Keenan Yonimine is a very high-level grappler who came from Enson and Egan Inoue's Grappling Unlimited and Pure Bred gym, who now trains under Tommy and also has Japan experience, and has won titles there.

We train at Tommy's school three times a week; Monday, Wednesday, and Saturday. I sprint and walk 4 miles with my dog up Makakilo Drive two times a week, Thursday and Friday, and continue my strength and conditioning drills at home at 4:00 am before I head out for work Tuesday, Thursday, and Friday. Sunday is rest. I spar and roll with some partners who are my weight for speed and because my opponent is younger than me and Tommy anticipates he will be stronger than me, so he has me work with partners heavier than me. We train in three five-minute rounds. My fight will be two three-minute rounds and all my teammates will be two five-minute rounds.

July through September 2008 would prove to be the longest Summer of my life. We leave Honolulu Wednesday morning October 15th and arrive in Narita Friday evening.

It's my first time in another country.

Being in one of the birthplaces of martial arts is a feeling I can't explain. I have trained the martial arts three-quarters of my life and read and learned from others about the Orient's martial arts beginnings. Some are accurate, some not so sure. To finally be here as a martial artist and go to battle here with one of their sons was surreal. As we walked out of the jetway, Tommy extended his hand out and said to me, "*Welcome to Japan!!!*" I looked at his hand for what seemed like a long time, then looked at him and smiled, shaking his hand. *I was ready.*

Sunday, October 19, 2008. Fight day.

I didn't get much sleep the night before, like all my competition bouts. We get to Tokyo Gold's gym where the tournament is held. The fight will be in a boxing ring. My fight will be the first fight for the Japan Submission Arts Wrestling Featherweight title. Behind the ring is a curtain with a large room where the fighters warm up. There is no divider between us. I can see my opponent hitting the mitts to warm up. He's whacking them pretty solid. I tell Keenan, "*Those psych-out games don't work on this old man,*" and he laughs.

The promoter is a former wrestling student of catch wrestling Karl Kotch. Hidetaka Aso, or *Aso Sensei*, as he is called, is walking where the fighters are. He is a Judo/Sambo/Catch Wrestler who has written books about his styles. He is tall and very brawn and has military basic training-style hair cut and wears a graying goatee. I approach him and extend my hand for a handshake and he gives me a cold stare and walks on. I realize later in Japan it is more proper to bow. What a dumbass I was.

It's time to go to war.

I walk up the stairs and bless myself with the sign of the cross and step through the ropes and enter the ring. All my teammates are with me in my corner. I feel strong and I feel my dad's spirit with me. I don't have any butterflies. I am wearing knee supports on both legs. Both knees started giving me pain when I was in my late 30s, but nothing chronic or disruptive in training or everyday life. When the bell rings I remember distinctly Shimizu instantly roundhouse-kicked my knee, not the outer thigh but my knee. His trainers must have instructed him to go for my legs thinking I have bad knees. It was a very solid shot which left me with a very big red welt the next day. I make him pay for the shot and I hit him with a hard right to the body simultaneously with a roundhouse kick. Because of my age, there are no headshots. I continually pound his body with punch combinations and a solid knee strike, but he keeps coming forward. The entire bout consisted of me throwing combinations to his body and Shimizu kicking my outer thigh, with me giving back inner and outer leg kicks. Shimizu took me down four times but was never able to get a finishing hold on me, escaping or stifling the attempted submissions. All that my teammates have taught me and trained me in Brazilian Ju-Jitsu had worked for me. All the people I trained with for this fight had better Ju-Jitsu than him. They prepared me well. He could not frustrate or finish me. When the bout was over and the decision was announced his hand was raised. His four takedowns had won it for him. I did not feel robbed or bitter, though I felt dejected. I felt I could have done better.

After the match, when I returned to the staging area, Aso Sensei approached me and extended his hand and said, *"Tavares San,"* muttered something in Japanese then shook my hand.

Tommy and Keenan would go on to win their title bouts. Tommy would submit his opponent with a rear naked choke in the second round. Keenan knocked out his opponent with a perfectly timed uppercut to the solar plexus - his opponent dropped on all fours gasping for air looking like he was struggling to breathe from every hole in his body, including his asshole. When the referee reached the count of six and his opponent was still on all fours, I knew there was no way that guy would rise. Keenan gave a true illustration that Kempo is the first way.

My other teammates suffered losses like myself, but they too fought hard tough matches against formidable fighters. Later, Aso Sensei took the Japan and Hawaii team out to eat. At dinner, the fight doctor, who is a Judo man and who was also 47 at the time, walked up to me and told me in broken English, *"You very brave man, good boxer."*

One of Tommy's fighters who lives in Japan and speaks fluent Japanese met us at the restaurant. I told him I wanted to speak with Shimizu and that I needed him to interpret for me. I told Shimizu it was a tough fight just as I expected and it was an honor to fight him and to fight in his country. One day I'll tell my granddaughter about my fight with him. He nodded and thanked me, then told me that I didn't punch like an old man!

It took me a long time to get over that loss. I trained hard. My mind was right and I felt good, and I realized later how much I learned from my martial arts brothers in preparation for that fight. Learning new techniques, and seeing how far I can push myself beyond my limits, even at age 47, and how I gained respect from the martial artists overseas.

Even though I lost the decision, I gained respect from the martial artists in Japan. I wanted the title but instead gained respect. Titles change hands eventually, but respect lives on. You cannot put a price on that. It was a very high point in my martial arts life, traveling to Japan at age 47 and testing my Hawaii Kempo skills along with my younger Kempo brothers. It was an honor to train and go to war with them. To me, they will always be champions.

Before the fight card starts. Author is pictured third from left.

Going to war with my Kempo Brothers.

The BJJ training my Kempo Unlimited brothers trained me for prepared me for everything and anything my opponent had.

Inside leg kick to Japan S.A.W. Featherweight champ Yasuhiro Shimizu.

In the tradition of the warrior, after the battle we celebrate.

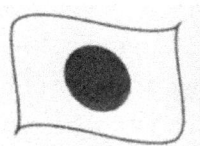 VS

JAPAN — U.S.A (HAWAII)

Red Corner   **Blue Corner**

<SAW・SPルール>

㉜ 清水靖弘
Y.SHIMIZU
(日本ウェルネススポーツ)
168cm/60kg　21歳

VS
(3分　2R)

㉝ **David Tavares**
ディビッド タバレス
(Kempo Unlimited Hi)
165cm/59kg　47歳

㉞ 光山将太
S.MITSUYAMA
(S.A.W)
170cm/70kg　23歳

VS
(5分　2R)

㉟ **Ryan Scoville**
ライアン スコビィリー
(Kempo Unlimited Hi)
173cm/70kg　28歳

㊱ 遠藤　隆
T.ENDO
(S.A.W)
179cm/92kg　41歳

VS
(5分　2R)

㊲ **Jeremy Wong**
ジェレミー ウォン
(Kempo Unlimited Hi)
185cm/110kg　34歳

㊳ 丸山　智
S.MARUYTAMA
(S.A.W)
168cm/87kg　30歳

VS
(5分　2R)

㊴ **Kynan Yonamine**
キーナン ヨナミネ
(Kempo Unlimited Hi)
170cm/81kg　34歳

㊵ 丸山航平
K.MARUYTAMA
(日本ウェルネススポーツ)
174cm/73kg　21歳

VS
(5分　2R)

㊶ **Tommy Lam**
トミー ラム
(Kempo Unlimited Hi)
175cm/68kg　35歳

2008 fight program from Tokyo, Japan

Walter Godin receives his coveted black belt from Adriano Emperado. This photo was illustrated in Fighting Arts Hawaii Magazine back in 2002 summer issue. It has since been disputed by many because of the black and white photo and the color of his belt is unknown. For the record the hand writing is that of Co-founder Frank Ordonez. You are welcomed to compare the handwriting if you have his signature on your certificate.

TOTAL RECALL

"You were born an original, don't die a copy."
-Portuguese Proverb

In the opinion of this author, the job of a martial arts instructor is to teach practical self-defense, and elite physical fitness, to teach the student to be individually thinking students, to instill respect, discipline, self-esteem, and a winning attitude in them, and apply it to everyday life. Train your black belts under you to teach the same way, to prepare them when they open a branch of your school, and maybe teach a little bit of history of the style or styles of your training. Black belts are teachers and leaders. They lead the students by example, no matter what rank they hold: Professor, Chief Instructor, or Head Instructor.

Martial artists have different goals, but the most sought-after goal is to become a black belt. Out of 100 students, one will make it to the black belt level in the most credible schools. Many won't have the discipline or fortitude to endure the grind of constant training or striving for the perfection of techniques. A black belt is paid for with time, pain, struggle, suffering, sacrifice, and experience. They chose the hard road and endured the tribulations of their training to earn the belt. Once they achieve the rank, it's up to them to prove their worth to uphold it and to be an example to the color belts and inspire them to achieve the same goal.

The subject I am about to address is one that I'm sure many have heard of or experienced in their martial arts life. Some may never have heard about it (but I doubt it) and some will deny it. This subject some instructors will disagree with me. Some will be neutral.

I mentioned a couple of paragraphs up that martial artists work hard and diligently to earn the coveted rank in any system. A rank they have earned. With many years of experience in achieving the rank, they picked up skills and knowledge that no one but God can take away.

There is a hard fact any instructor has to face: the possibility a black belt student may leave the school one day, on good terms or bad, to start their system or just over time have a fallout with their instructor. Or for many other different reasons. Whatever the case may be, they have earned the rank they wear. The instructor must have thought the idea was good or they would never have promoted them, but when the student decides to leave the school, to some instructors suddenly, the student is not a black belt anymore and wants the rank and certificate back. If Professor Chow wore a white belt after leaving Mitose's school, would his skills be that of a white belt? According to some instructors, the belt is his. The martial artist is only a black belt if you're under him and him only.

I know of two instructors who sent certified letters to their black belts when they left their school. The letter stated to return HIS belt and certificate and immediately stop teaching his techniques. For me if my student leaves my school and is still teaching my techniques, I would think that is a good thing because it would tell me that I must be teaching an effective system. A martial arts instructor had a black belt student leave his school. He wrote a certified letter to that student to return his rank and certificate. In time, that instructor had three black belts leave his school and he ended up writing the same letter to them that his instructor originally wrote. He was a robot. His mind was conditioned and controlled to act and become what he had left.

If a black belt leaves an organization for whatever the circumstances I can see if the instructor tells him he is not recognized as an instructor in that organization, but to demand back rank and certificate, to me is just plain childish, selfish, and foolish. When things like this happen in our system or any system, it gets me thinking, "What do these instructors want out of their students and the art? Control!" I am sure the majority of instructors do not feel that way although two instructors that I know have had a similar experience of that nature. These instructors never demanded back what the student earned.

Professor Godin told me about how people in the Kajukenbo system say that Professor Emperado had taken away his belt and certificate when he was booted out of Kajukenbo. The reason he was canned from Kajukenbo is a very long drawn-out story that I can talk about another time having a beer and a cigar in back yard martial arts talk. Godin said black belts were telling him Adriano wanted him to return the belt and certificate. Godin worked as a security guard at the Civic Auditorium where boxing fight cards took place and Emperado frequented the boxing matches, so Godin brought his certificate and belt with him to work at the next fight card. When he saw Adriano he gave it back. Professor Emperado asked him, *"What's this for?"*

"Everyone told me you wanted it back," Godin replied.

Emperado shook his head and told Godin, *"Get out of here, I don't want that."*

Godin smiled and left.

To this day, the majority of the Kajukenbo stylists think Godinv returned his rank to Sijo Adriano. Some even say he's not a black belt.

Now if a man like Professor Emperado, who was one of the founders of a hybrid system, acknowledges his student's accomplishment and lets him keep what's rightfully his, who are these guys to demand back rank?

Feliciano Ferriera had told me he had black belts leave his school. He told me about it when I ran into him and his wife Kiko at Ala Moana shopping center. I knew Feliciano for many years. When I was in high school he just came back from the Vietnam war a few years prior, a decorated hero. He received his black belt from another Kempo system, but Godin acknowledged his rank (and skill) and let him wear his belt in training. Feliciano is the type of guy I can ask him any question and he'll answer it, although you might not like the answer. I had to ask him if he asked for his student's rank back after they left.

He frowned at me and answered *"Shit no! It's theirs, they got black belt skills, and they ain't no scrubs."*

I didn't ask any more questions.

I feel the need to address this issue that goes on in our art. To me, this is not the Kempo or Kajukenbo way, or the spirit of the martial arts. If you have experienced your instructor asking for HIS rank back, give it back to him. If he honestly believes that rank is given and not *earned* then you don't need an instructor with that kind of character or any association with that kind of controlling mindset.

Head instructor Jenna Koseki and 8th degree Professor Tommy Lam of the Kempo Unlimited schools present Brett Arizumi his black belt after a very hard and draining test.

EFFECTIVE KEMPO/KAJUKENBO STREET-DEFENSE

"Self-Defense is not just a set of techniques, but a state of mind. And it begins with the belief that you are worth defending."
-Rorion Gracie

A hoodlum will attack their victims only one way - as a coward. They will prey upon those they believe will not be a threat to them, and they will attack in numbers, unexpectedly, or with a weapon. The Kempo/Kajukenbo fighting style was developed primarily for street combat first, and competition second. This self-defense segment is not intended to show the superiority of one method over another but to show the continuing refinement of the Kempo/Kajukenbo art, by the men who have withstood the test of time and have dedicated their method to the art of combat.

The following instructors offer their blend of self-defense techniques at the highest level of martial arts. Each man comes from a lineage that is deeply rooted in Kempo and Kajukenbo Hawaii history.

DAVID DUCAY

Name: David Ducay

Age: 56

Years Training: 43

Style: Kajukenbo

Lineage: Professor Bautista/ Professor Ramos Method

Crossed trained: Jeet Kune Do (Hartsell, Bustillio, Inosanto) Doce Pares Eskrima, Gracie BJJ, Muay Thai, Boxing, MMA Wrestling, Kali (Dan Inosanto)

Rank: 8th Degree Senior Professor (Kajukenbo)

6th Grade Master (Doce Pares/Eskrido/ Escrima

Co-Founder Kajukenbo/Escrima

School: Bautista Kajukenbo Self-Defense Institute, Vallejo, Ca.

Noted Black Belts: Renel Amante, Mike Richie, Jerry Corpus, Vince Williams, Larry Amante.

Affiliations: KSDI, Kajukenbo-Escrima Corpus Schools (Advisor), UFMAC, JCMA.

Escape from a front bear hug

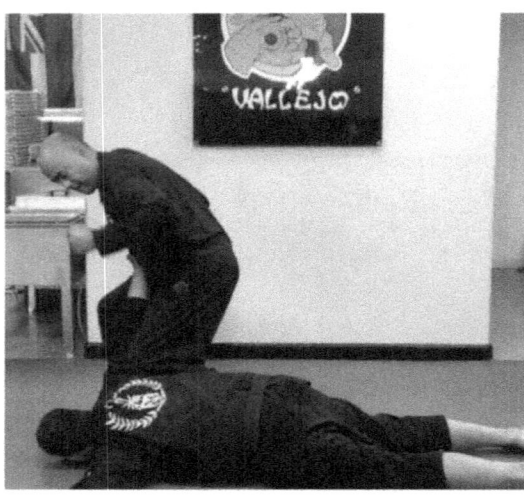
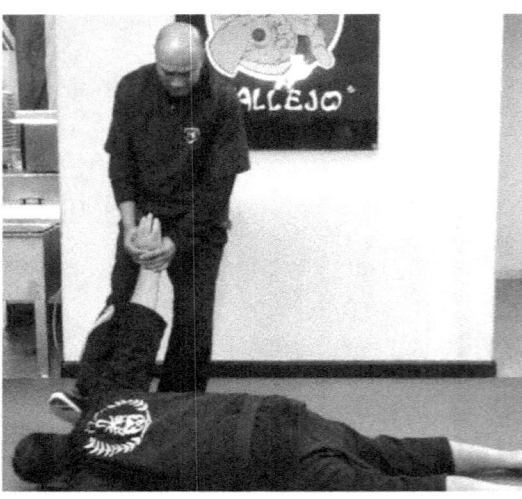

Escape from a rear bear hug

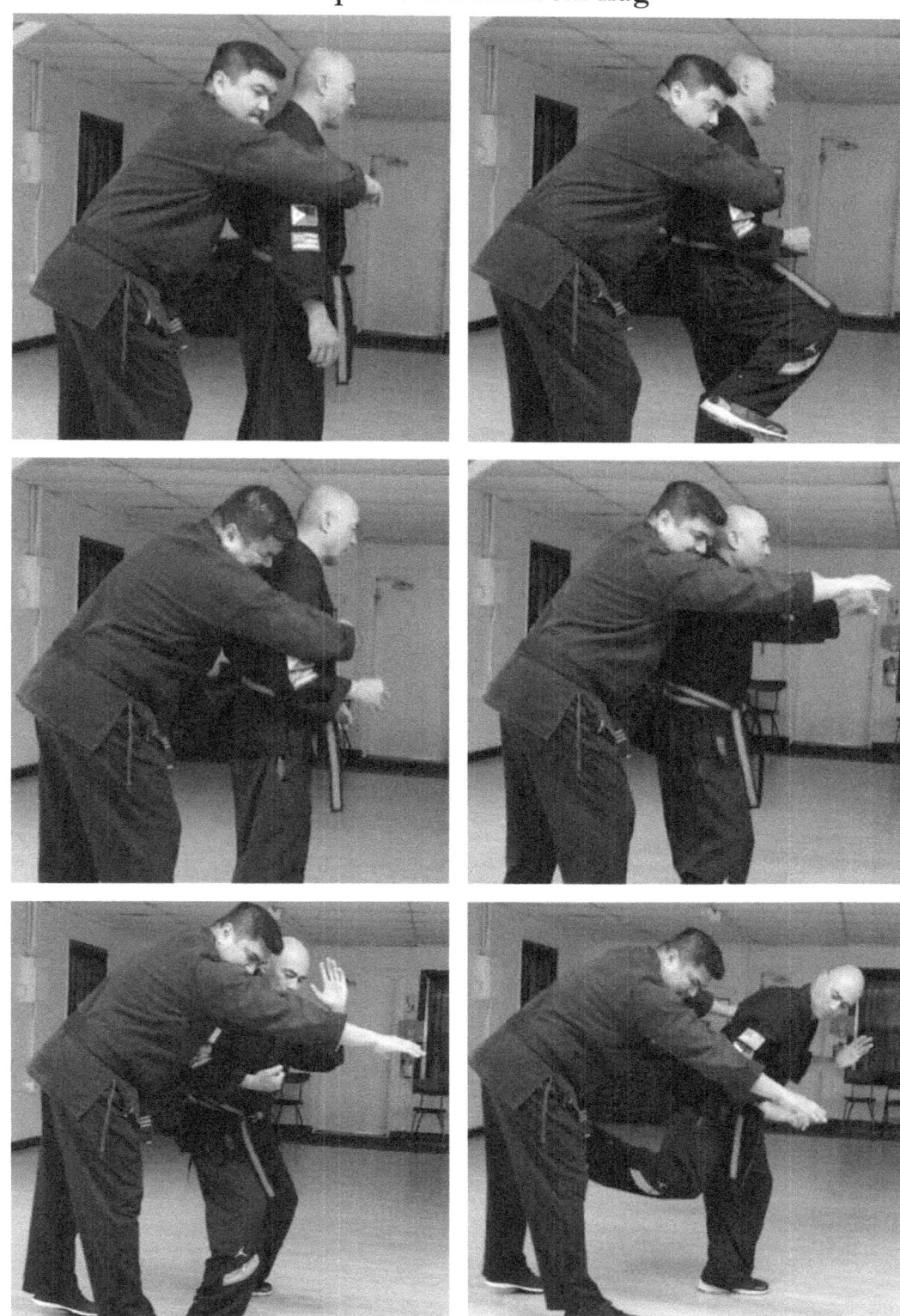

Escape from rear bear hug continued

ANDREW EVANS

Name: Andrew Evans

Age: 47

Years Training: 32

Style: Kempo/Kajukenbo

Lineage: Professor Walter Godin

Crossed Trained: Modern Arnis (Remy Presas), Kung Fu, Boxing, Vee Arnis Jitsu (John Petrone), Natural Spirit International (Kelly Worden), Scientific Fighting Congress (Hock Hochheim) Matsubayashi Shorin Ryu (Ruben West).

Rank: 7th Degree (Kempo) 6th Degree (Kajukenbo) 5th Degree Kara Zen Po Go Shin-Jitsu, 2nd Degree Modern Arnis.

School: Hokkien Martial Arts, Topeka Kansas

Noted Black Belts: Sheryl Barber (5th Degree), William Barngrover (1st Degree) Michael Fisher (Student Black Belt)

Afilliations: Ordonez Kajukenbo Ohana, KSDI

Escape from one hand wrist grab

Escape from two-hand wrist grab

JASON GROFF

Name: Jason Groff

Age: 56

Years Training: 48

Style: Kajukenbo

Lineage: Frank Ordonez Kajukenbo Co-Founder

Crossed Trained: Judo, (Homestead AFB, Fl) Hapkido (Musan Korea) Muay Thai, Kru-Trainer (Chonburi, Thailand), Kali-Escrima (Angeles, P.I.)

Special Self-Defense Instruction: Police Defense Tactics (Master Instructor) Pearl Harbor, Hawaii 1991.

Rank: 9th Degree Red/Silver Belt

Title: Grandmaster

School: Ordonez Kajukenbo Ohana Headquarters Wahiawa, Hawaii

Noted Black Belts: Lee Hines, Emory Hicks, Ron Baker, Gavin Tsuda, Waiele McMillian, and Matt Yandora.

Affiliations: Ordonez Kajukenbo Ohana (Senior Advisor)

Counter-to-punch attack

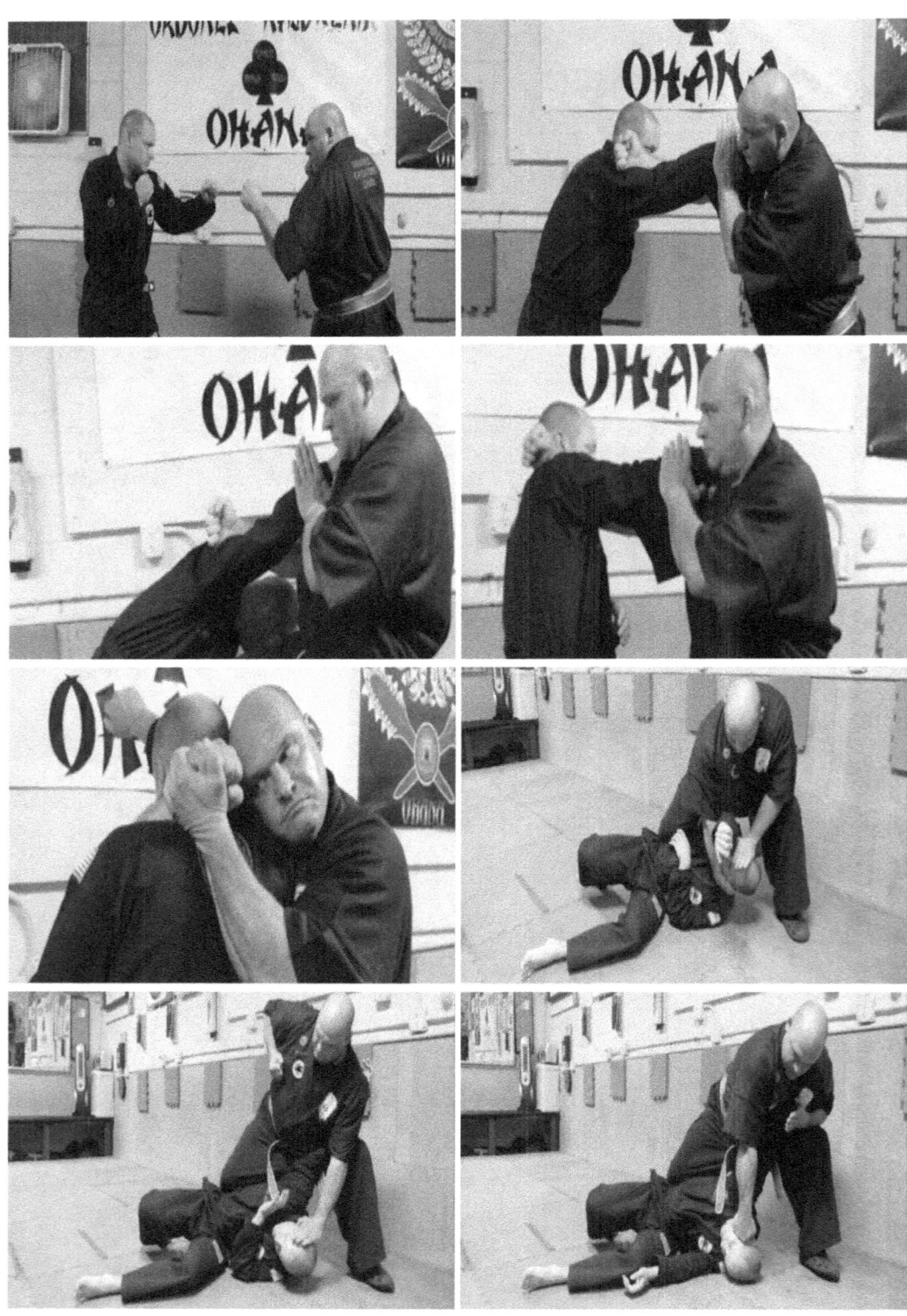

Escape from a front bear hug

DAVID KOVAR

Name: David Kovar

Age: 58

Years Training: 45

Style: American Kenpo

Lineage: Grandmaster Al Tracy

Cross Trained: Kosho Ryu (Mitose), Tae Kwon Do (Jhoon Rhee), Jeet Kune Do (Burton Richardson), Serrada Escrima (George Santana), Doce Pares (Nito Noval), Iaido and Kobudo (Mikio Nishiuchi), Degergerg Blend (Fred Degerberg), Brazilian Ju-Jitsu (Carlos Valente and Pedro Sauer).

Rank: 8th Degree

School: The Satori Alliance Sacramento, CA.

Noted Black Belts: Ken Grube 6th Degree, Mark Caswell 6th Degree, Chad Shepherd 5th Degree, Nick Wilson 5th Degree, Gordon Schroeder 5th Degree.

Counter-to-punch attack

Escape from two hand grab attack

TOMMY LAM

Name: Tommy Lam

Age: 44

Years Training: 35

Style: Kempo/Kajukenbo

Lineage: Professor Walter Godin/ Co-Founder of Kajukenbo Frank Ordonez

Crossed trained: Brazilian Ju-Jujitsu (Relson Gracie Uptown, Egan Inoue), Boxing, Judo, Muay Thai, Gung Fu (Hung Gar system)

Rank: 8th Degree (Kempo) 8th Degree (Kajukenbo), 7th Degree (Submission Arts Wrestling Federation)

Titles: 1995 San Shou Kung Fu Lightweight Champion, 2-time HKL Sport Ju-Jitsu Lightweight gold medalist, 2-time Canadian Tiger Balm International international Sport Ju-Jitsu lightweight silver medalist, 2003 Canadian Tiger Balm International, Lightweight Sport Ju-Jitsu gold medalist, 2005 and 2008 Submission Arts Wrestling Federation Japan Lightweight Champion, 2010 IBJ/SAW Federation Japan Lightweight Champion.

School: Kempo Unlimited, Honolulu, Hawaii

Noted Black Belts: Danny Lam, Jenna Koseki, John Rebudal, Todd Nakamua, Jeremy Wong, Brett Arizumi, Allyson Kuwana, and Sheldon Tokuda

Affiliations: Ordonez Kajukenbo Ohana, Submission Arts Wrestling Federation

Escape from a knife attack

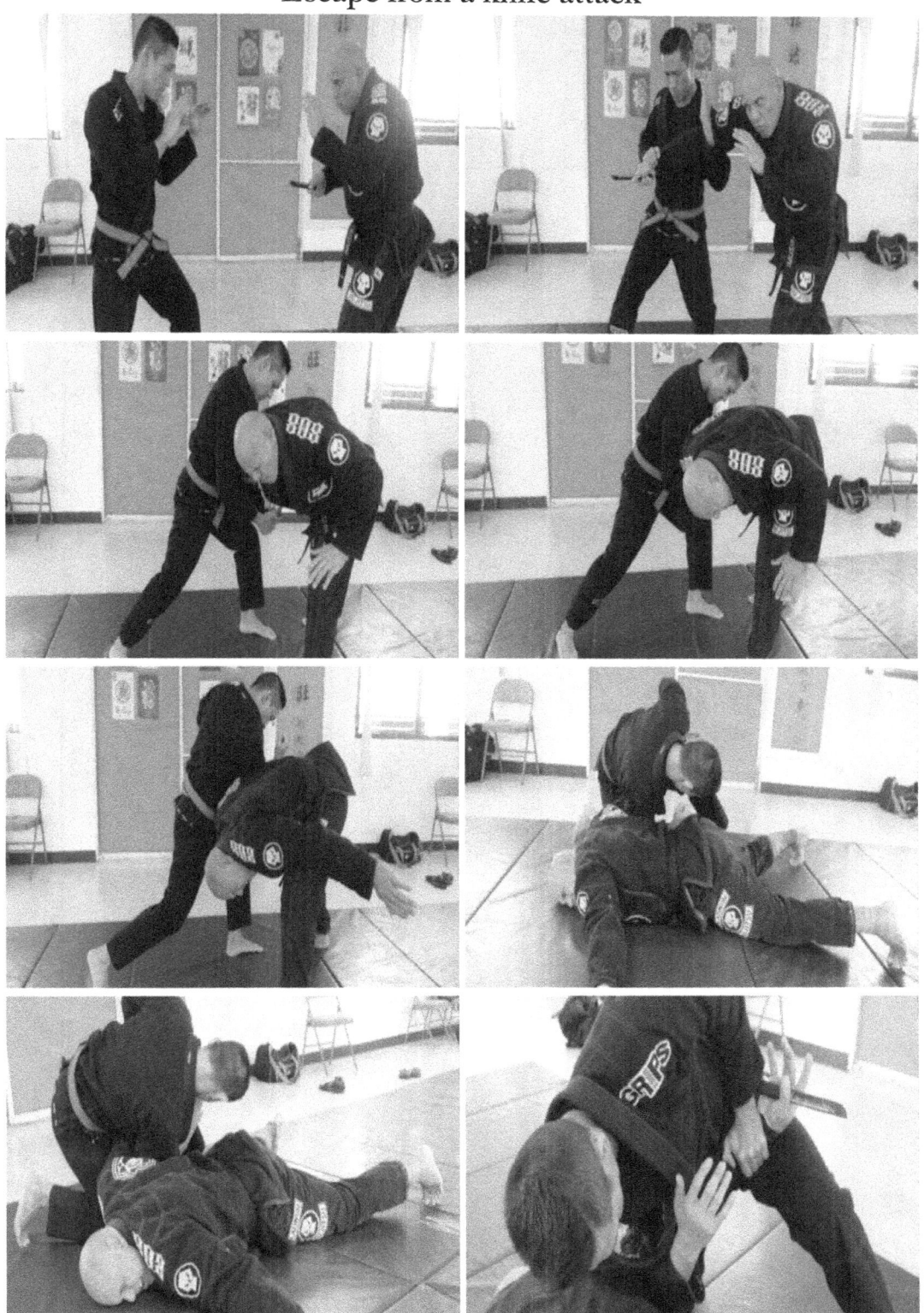

Escape from grab punch attack

FRANK ROBELLO

Name: Frank Robello

Age: 48

Years Training: 28

Style: Kempo/Kajukenbo

Lineage: Professor Johnathan Vance

Crossed Trained: Boxing, Kick Boxing, Aikido

Rank: 8th Degree (Kempo-Karate), 8th Degree (Kajukenbo)

School: Advanced Kempo-Karate System, Pacific Palisades, Hawaii

Noted Black Belts: George Versola III (8th Degree), Don Kawabata, Albert Rosario, Brent Hamasaki, Lance Ushida.

Afilliations: Ordonez Kajukenbo Ohana

Defense against a knife attack

Escape from a club attack

FINAL THOUGHTS

"The martial arts are based upon understanding hard work, and total comprehension of skills."
-Bruce Lee

"The way is in training," Kyokushin and BJJ stylist Marco Lala quoted in his book <u>The Ultimate Weapon</u>.

That's the way I see martial arts.

When I opened my school in 1996, I spoke with a martial artist whom I considered a friend and a person whose opinion I respected. He brought up the subject of rank and asked me who would promote me now that I am no longer affiliated with any Kempo organization. I told him I didn't care and I would promote myself. He replied that my rank would not be legitimate because no one legitimately promoted me, and therefore no one in the martial arts community would recognize it. I explained that there are many high-ranking black belts that promoted themselves. He answered that they have big schools and have many black belts under them and are well known in the Kempo and martial arts community, so people recognize and accept their rank.

I realized that this guy's mindset was the same as his instructor's. At one time, I taught at his instructor's school for six years but eventually I left that school. This guy had left that instructor's school earlier and later went back, only to leave again.

I concluded: to him and his instructor, martial arts were about rank.

Period!

Not too long after that conversation I was talking to a Gracie Ju-Jitsu practitioner who was also a co-worker. We were discussing martial arts, and the subject of rank came up. He said he read an article about Frank Shamrock talking about the black belt rank. Frank, at that time, was at the height of his MMA career, submitting and defeating many opponents, BJJ black belts as well, and Frank held no rank in BJJ or any submission martial art at that time. Frank stated that he would choose skill, experience, and exceptional training as well as physical fitness over having a black belt anytime.

That remark always stuck in my head.

I remembered my childhood martial arts idol Bruce Lee never held any legitimate black belt in any system, but his skills and physique are undeniably second to none, pound for pound, and people to this day respect and recognize his martial arts abilities.

I am in no way putting myself in the same class as Frank Shamrock or Bruce Lee, but my philosophy is the same as theirs. There is no substitution for training, experience, and skill. You either do it, have it, or don't.

In July 2001, a month before he passed away, Professor Godin promoted me to 5th degree at his summer martial arts tournament at Palama Gym - 30 years and one month into my training. After the promotion the same guy whose opinion I once respected came up to me and told me I was lucky to be promoted by Professor Godin.

I started my training in June of 1971 just a month shy of my 10th birthday. Throughout the years of training I thought by winning a lot of local and international tournaments would make me the best martial artist.

I fell short many times. Fighting and losing many tough matches and I was pretty hard on myself. In time I realized that it was the hard training and preparation for the fights, and learning to respect my opponents through the wars, that made me a better martial artist and a better man. Constant learning and rough roads brought me to a higher level in martial arts and life. You can't take the easy road and expect to get better. Constantly fill your cup of knowledge. Humility is a big part of martial arts that many vain martial artists forget about.

I am not a well-known or celebrated Kempo warrior, but I and the martial artists that I train with and the people I have written about in this book and the past are PROGRESSING martial artists. **We do not HOLD rank. We strive to UPHOLD the rank we have EARNED.** We will continue to do so until we aren't able to. Every martial artist I wrote about in this book has achieved extraordinary accomplishments in the arts. They put it all on the line at one time or another, be it in the ring, on the streets, or pioneering their particular style and going against the grain and introducing their art to a different part of the world.

Anyone can open a school, watch tapes, go to a few seminars then teach it to their students and pawn it off as their own, and be a number counting paper pusher while holding a high rank and having their students worship them like some fire-breathing demigod. Being promoted by Professor Godin was a crowning achievement, but my journey to the rank was more important to me.

This 46-year martial arts journey was an educating one. I realized how fortunate I was to have trained in the arts and to have met the people I have trained with over the years.

Like life, I see the high points and the low points, and I take each as a learning lesson. I met some lifelong friends through the martial arts, from icons to martial arts celebrities, and unfortunately (or maybe fortunately) I've met some martial artists who think very highly of themselves and ONLY of themselves. I have seen effective methods and I have seen absolute pure shit, both of which helped me gauge instructors as an artist and as men. I've spoken and debated with others about their art and their views. I learned just how much I love and missed training and learning martial arts when I would be away for periods because of work. But always kept it in my soul. I love talking about it, writing about it, and writing about the people who train it and learn life's lessons through it.

Every day is a battle, and God and Kempo gave me the inner strength to overcome my obstacles and learn from them and strive to take life and training to higher levels. I believe martial arts, like all science, should evolve. Like the great Bruce Lee once said, *"Respect tradition, but don't be bound by it."*

Through it all I've learned two things: I'm blessed and "lucky."

Much mahalo for buying this book. May God bless you and keep you. I expect to receive a lot of feedback about this book, and most I believe will be backlash. My instructor, Professor Walter L.N. Godin, was the most controversial figure in the Kempo and Kajukenbo world, and after writing this book, I'll probably be the second most controversial figure in Kempo and Kajukenbo.

Aloha! Keep training, keep teaching!

Summer 2004. Getting an ass-kicking at John Hackleman's Pit. Notice I'm the same size as Ice Man and Lighty. This was after Hackleman was inducted into the KSDI Hall Of Fame.

UFC welterweight contender Jason "Mayhem" Miller schooled all of us on the mat at Kempo Unlimited.

Myself and my students learning small circle Ju-Jitsu from Wally Jay at Kempo Unlimited, 1996

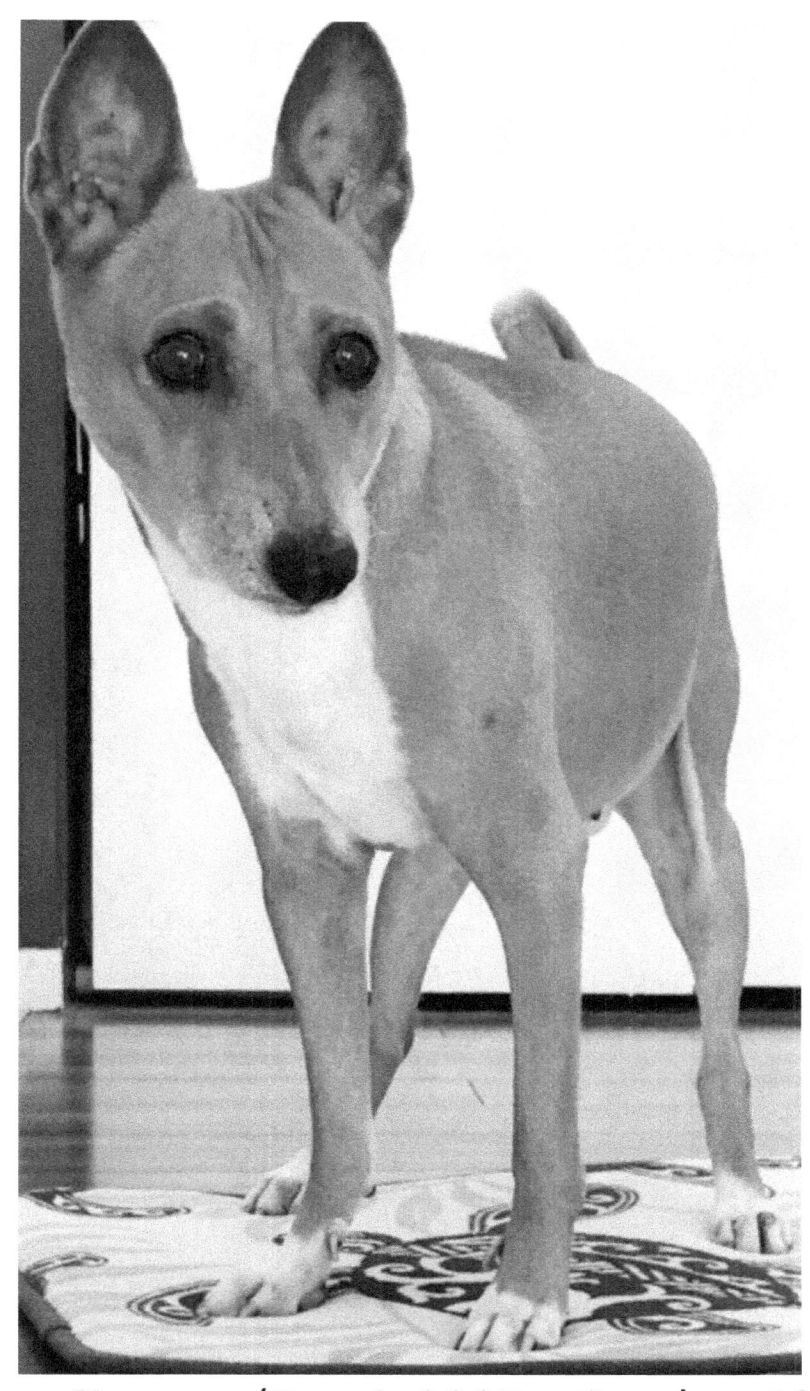

Bruce Lee Tavares (Dec 4, 2007 – October 13, 2022)

In loving memory of my pal, my son, Bruce Lee Tavares. December 4th, 2007 - October 13, 2022. In 2008 you ran up Makakilo Drive hill with me to help me prepare for my fight against Yasuhiro Shimizu San. I realize now, son, you were pushing me so that I would be in my best physical shape. Aloha Ke Akua. Until we run again. Love you, Dad

ABOUT THE AUTHOR

David Tavares is an 8th Degree Tavares Chinese Kempo/ 8th Degree Ordonez Kajukenbo Ohana. He started his martial arts training in June 1971 at the Godin's School of Self-Defense Pacific Palisades branch in Pearl City, Hawaii. He served three years in the United States Army as a combat engineer in the 1st Cavalry Division 8th Engineer Battalion. Fort Hood, Texas 1979-1982.

1983 USA/ABF Hawaii State Flyweight Boxing Champion

1989 Ted Tabura's Festival of the King's Lightweight Champion. (Lahaina, Maui)

1998 Shaolin Kung Fu championships continuous fighting Lightweight gold medalist. (Chinatown, Honolulu Hawaii)

1998 American Black Belt Championships continuous fighting silver medalist (Santa Barbra, Ca)

Writer of the DVD "What is Chinese Kempo?"

Former owner and editor of Fighting Arts Hawaii magazine

Fought in a pro-MMA bout in 2008 at age 47 in Tokyo, Japan on the Submission Arts Wrestling Japan vs. Hawaii fight card

Received his 5th-degree black belt from Professor Godin in July 2001

Received his 8th degree from Kajukenbo Co-founder Frank Ordonez in January 2012

Retired Oil Refinery mechanic for 25 years (1991-2017)

Licensed Massage Therapist in the state of Hawaii

David lives in Makakilo Heights, on the island of Oahu. He has a daughter, three grandchildren, and a Basenji dog named Bruce Lee.

He can be contacted by email at **fightingarts@msn.com** or online at http://www.Black-Robe.net

Stone Compass Press specializes in paperback and eBook publishing with a focus on Science Fiction, Metaphysical, Esoteric, Paranormal, Hawaiiana and Educational genres.

Take your first steps to a successful writing career at www.StoneCompassPress.com.

We offer some of the highest royalties in the USA!
$0 up front costs* (*complete eBook manuscripts only)

Phone: 808.238.2264 | Email: stonecompasspress@gmail.com

Also from Stone Compass Press

Maui Vortex Field Guide
(Zach Royer, 2019)

Hawai'i Vortex Field Guide
(Zach Royer, 2014)

Why Are We Here on Earth?
(Michael W. Evrard, 2022)

Pyramid Rising: Planetary Acupuncture to Combat Climate Change
(Zach Royer, 2012)

Web design, brand recognition, business services & more at www.ZOAT.org

2023 Sponsored Page Rates

Feature your business with a sponsored page in this book!

FULL PAGE
4.5" X 7.5"

~~$250~~

$200

*Price displayed is for our 3-month quarterly rate.

Learn more or purchase a sponsorship at www.StoneCompassPress.com/advertising